THERE IS

LIFE AFTER

WHAT'S-HIS-

NAME

ISBN 0-9773939-0-9
ISBN 0-9773939-1-7 (ebook)

Published by Pinnacle Thought, Inc.

Printed in the United States of America

Interior production and copyediting by Martha Nichols/aMuse Productions

There Is Life After What's-His-Name

Susan Russo

Dedication

I DEDICATE THIS BOOK TO MY MOM WHO HAS BEEN THERE for me through all of the good times and the bad. Your constant love and support has been unwavering and I have always found solace in knowing that I could turn to you.

To my family and friends: Your presence is a reminder of the fortune I've amassed in love, compassion, and memories. Thank you for being a part of my life.

Acknowledgments

TO MY NIECE AND EDITOR ANNIE, I CAN'T THANK YOU enough for helping me read and edit my book. Your sense of humor and little comments will never be forgotten.

To James for always answering your cell phone — and I also want to thank all of my friends who listened and for those of you who gave me the input to make it possible.

And a special thanks to Martha Nichols from aMuse Productions for adding the finishing touches; your help and support were the icing on the cake.

Contents

Introduction

I HAVE THOUGHT LONG AND HARD ABOUT WHY I DECIDED to write this book since I would be entering into a world that doesn't favor unpublished authors and I don't have the ever-so-helpful *Ph.D.* after my name. I wrote it because I know what it is like to be in an unhealthy relationship and stay when I knew I should've gotten out. I wrote it because I know there are a lot of people who are suffering in the same sort of relationships and who just need that final bit of encouragement or that little nudge that will help them to make the crucial first step forward and walk away from a bad relationship. I've also observed many people struggling hopelessly through the "letting-go" process after their relationships were over, and I wanted to provide them with the tools to move on.

I know first-hand how difficult it is to walk away. I know how you will rationalize any kind of behavior to justify your staying. But I also know that when you choose to stay it is very damaging to your self-esteem. I wanted to write this book for those of you who are teetering on the edge of knowing you should leave but feeling you can't and also for those who hope there just has to be a better life out there. I wrote this book to tell you that there unequivocally is another life, and it will be better if you take the initiative and move on.

I also wanted to impart to you the single most important factor in making your life better and to help keep you from making the same mistakes again: *You must take the time and put forth the energy to learn how to love yourself more*, thereby raising your self-esteem. This is the number one key in living a healthier life. No one else can make a difference but you.

You may not believe it right now, but you have the power to take your life in any direction you choose. Quit driving your destiny down dead end streets and head out to the highway of life. You know what they say: "Get a life." Just make sure it's a good life!

I want you to know that, for me, the road hasn't always been easy, but all of the hard lessons I have gone through are worth the person I am today. My greatest hope in writing this book is to make a difference in your life if you are unnecessarily suffering in a bad relationship. My desire is to give you that extra bit of courage to make a change not only in your situation but more importantly in how you view yourself.

I sincerely hope the lessons in this book will enable you to take the first step forward so you can at least have a chance at a better future and allow yourself the opportunity to have a more fulfilling life.

Part One

KNOWING
WHEN TO LEAVE

_____Chapter One_____

Should I Stay
or Should I Leave?

Advice is what we ask for when we already know the
answer but wish we didn't.

— *Erica Jong*

HOW MANY TIMES IN THE PAST SIX MONTHS HAVE YOU
asked yourself, "Should I stay or should I leave?" You wouldn't be
asking yourself this question if you were in a happy, healthy relationship. Have you ever known of anyone in a great relationship with a
loving, respectful, and giving man who asked herself, "I wonder if I
should leave?" The fact that you are even asking this question is your
answer! Don't be one of the many women who are discontented and
stay in unsatisfying, unfulfilling relationships.

This book is a survivor's guide to breaking out of unhealthy relationships: the kind that come fraught with either disappointment, disrespect, inconsideration, distrust, indifference, or a lot of other stuff that
doesn't make you feel good. You know when you are in an unhealthy
relationship — when you are unhappy most of the time.

You fight a lot; cry a lot; feel depressed; question whether you
really are as screwed up as he says you are; second-guess what you

say or do; wonder if it really is all your fault; question his honesty, his integrity, his commitment; and you just plain feel bad. You constantly struggle with trying to make "this kind" of relationship work. It's a sad, frustrating, never-ending battle. If only you could give up and walk away.

Guess what? *You can!*

If you are trying to decide whether you should stay or leave, think about why you bought this particular book in the first place. Every relationship has its ups and downs, strengths and weaknesses; that's normal. You have to work at having a good, healthy relationship. You compromise, you work at communicating your feelings, and you learn to listen. There are times when you are the giver and he's the receiver and vice versa. It's a mutual give and take, each person wanting to do whatever it takes to make things right.

The key here is that *both* partners want it to work and are willing to put forth the effort to make it work. These relationships have a solid foundation, and when a problem does arise (which they always do in any relationship), given a little bit of time and energy, the relationship will be back on track. These are not the kind of relationships we will be discussing. Are you really in a healthy relationship, struggling with normal ups and downs, or are you in an unhealthy relationship, wondering why you are so unhappy most of the time?

Too many people are living unhappy lives. They accept it as their lot in life — as if this is the hand life has dealt them, without any awareness as to how they can make a change in their lives. Or they simply don't believe they have the power to change.

Some people are paralyzed by fear. They are afraid of change. They would rather stay where they are, bad relationship and all, because at least they *know* what they have. Their fear of the unknown will keep them stuck in a rut. How do you want to live your life? With someone who doesn't really care for you the way you need or want to be cared for? Do you really believe you don't deserve more? And are you willing to settle for less from life than what you have every right to achieve?

Ask yourself: Are you a better person for knowing him? Does he enrich your life? Is this how you always thought it would be? Does he bring out the best in you? Do you feel as if you are one of the lucky ones? Is he the kind of partner you'd choose for your daughter or a friend? If the answers are no, then *don't settle for any less than what you want and deserve*!

Begin today. Do some homework. Get to know yourself. Learn to love yourself and take care of the little girl in you. Take the time and expend the energy. Go for it. You *are* worth it — you just may not know it yet.

If you'll give yourself the chance — if you'll walk away from what is causing you so much pain, grief, and aggravation, and learn to love yourself more — you will begin to effect a change in your life that I know will be positive.

As they say, "Life is short," so make it the best that it can be. You and you alone possess the power to take your future in any direction you choose.

Chapter Two

Haven't You Had Enough?

Death is not the greatest loss in life. The greatest loss is what dies inside us while we live.

— *Norman Cousins*

OKAY, YOU ARE IN A RELATIONSHIP THAT YOU KNOW ISN'T making you happy. More than likely it's some kind of disrespectful behavior that is causing you to feel you want to leave. Now what *exactly* is this man doing (or not doing) that would make you think you don't want to put up with it anymore? Everyone's circumstances are different, but just stay with me for a minute.

Focus on the behavior that you don't want to live with anymore. Focus on what makes you feel bad, frustrates you, or makes you hurt. Would you ever, for one second, allow your best friend (or anyone else for that matter) to treat you the same way? Would you tolerate even half of it? Then why in the world would you allow this man, who says he "loves" you, to treat you as he does? How many times would you let a friend treat you like this without saying, "Enough is enough; I don't need friends like you." But for some reason, you tolerate the intolerable…and you do it over and over again. Why?

Obviously, because you don't truly believe that you deserve better — and if that's the case, you don't know how very wrong you are! You are a *wonderful* person, and you deserve to have happiness and fulfillment in your life. If you don't understand that, I strongly recommend a therapist to help you get your self-worth back on track. Or at least you should read books to help you learn how to love yourself and raise your self-esteem.

Beginning to love and respect yourself is the single most important step in making a change in your situation. Would you ever just stand back and watch while a person hurt someone you love? Well, that "someone" happens to be you. If you love yourself, you will protect yourself. Once you learn how to truly love yourself, you won't allow others to hurt you, and you won't continually attract the kind of people who make you feel unlovable. Loving yourself is where it all begins.

I know you've heard the saying that only a crazy person continues to do the same thing expecting a different outcome. I know first-hand. I've been there. I even took it one step further by trying different tactics to change him or change his behavior and had the same outcomes: hurt, frustration, disappointment, and disillusionment. It took me a long time to learn that I can't change anyone but myself nor should I feel it is my right to.

However, what you do have the right to do is to honestly and seriously voice your concerns and issues. Only then you will see whether your words fall on deaf ears or if your feelings are duly noted and at least taken into consideration to make a change in the future.

My friend Julie eventually woke up to this fact after months of trying to be heard — by crying, screaming, and yelling at her boyfriend. She finally sat down with Mr. No-I-Won't-Compromise and explained to him that if he continued not coming home after work without even the courtesy of a phone call, she would be gone. (The secret here is saying it and meaning it.) She further went on to explain to him that she wasn't going to try to change him anymore. If he wanted to stay out all night that was his choice but he needed to realize that all of our choices come with consequences and the consequence here was that she was going to leave. His selfishness simply didn't work for her anymore. Thankfully, Julie came to the realization that the only thing she could change was what *she* was willing to accept.

It doesn't feel good when you're the only one trying to make a difference in your relationship. Are you the one doing all the compromising and making all the concessions? Let's face it, none of us is perfect, but I'm not discussing imperfection here. I'm talking about indifference, disrespect, inconsideration, emotional or physical abuse, or whatever your personal circumstance. How many times do you have to feel bad before you leave? How many times do you have to be disappointed, rejected, put down, yelled at, hit, ignored, or embarrassed before you wake up and say, "I've had enough!"

Nobody deserves to be treated badly, not even you. You really owe it to yourself to seek happiness and fulfillment, not sadness and emptiness. Not that you are actually seeking sadness and emptiness, but you've found it and you won't let go of it. Even though it's not healthy for you, it's familiar and comfortable. You are living in your comfort zone. To learn more about your comfort zone, read Peter McWilliams's book, *Do it...Get Off Your Buts*.

So now is the time to pick yourself up by the boot straps, get to know what is really important to you in a relationship, and get to know and like yourself better so you can find someone who appreciates you. There are a lot of men out there who are loving and supportive, fun to be with, and actually want a good relationship. Don't waste anymore time with Mr. Wrong.

A whole new world is open to you — a new life. But remember, the number one key to finding the right man is to begin to know how really valuable *you* are.

It's called your self-worth. It's worth discovering.

Chapter Three

How Does He Value You?
Let Me Count the Ways

One must always tell what one sees. Above all, which is more difficult, one must always see what one sees.
— Charles Peguy

YOU'RE THINKING ABOUT LEAVING HIM FOR A REASON, and my guess is that the reasons are many — but I know from experience that in some cases, the reasons can be few. Even if it's only for one reason, it can be so big, so monumental, that it's causing you to want to end it. For instance, he may be wonderful in many ways, but his gambling or alcoholism is destroying your relationship. Whatever your circumstances are, when you're sitting there thinking you might be making a mistake, think back on the last three to six months or the last year.... What does he do to make you feel valued or not valued? What does he do to try to make things work?

Has he been respectful? Has he been affectionate (outside of wanting to fulfill his own needs)? Does he compromise, or is it 'his way or the highway'? Does he listen to you? Does he care what you think or feel, or is his opinion the only one that matters? Has he been romantic in any little way? Does he appreciate you? Does he tell you he loves you? Has he even come close to treating you like he did in the beginning?

Remember, *actions speak louder than words*. So if you were wondering if he's the man of your dreams, wonder no more. If you are not getting what you want from this relationship, why stay?

My friend Jessica was in a good relationship with a man she called her soul mate. He was fifteen years older than she was. He bought her a business, they traveled together, he doted on her, rubbed her back every night, and she said she loved how comfortable she could be around him. We were having a conversation about my book, and she surprised me by saying, "I understand. I ask myself at least two or three times a week if I should leave." I was shocked. I said, "I thought you were happy." Well, she was — except for the issues concerning his eleven-year-old daughter and jealous ex-wife.

Anytime the ex called, he jumped. If an argument started while he was on the phone with the ex, it changed his mood and ruined the evening. Jessica thought the marriage had ended two years ago, but at times he acted like he was still in it. Then there was the issue of his daughter — a child with absolutely no discipline can wreak havoc on your life, particularly when it's not your child. His daughter was disrespectful and seemed to intentionally do things to offend my friend. Not only did he ignore his daughter's obnoxious behavior, but if Jessica would try to address the topic, he didn't want to hear it and he refused to do anything about it.

There are a lot of reasons you can use to talk yourself into staying in an unhappy relationship. Of course, most of these reasons are clouded by your emotions. But there is one very good reason why you shouldn't — because you owe yourself the truth. You are not happy, and you haven't been happy for a long time. You know you've tried to make him understand how you feel but he just doesn't get it. Don't second-guess yourself; you've been wanting to leave for a reason.

Another friend of mine was stuck in a relationship that wasn't making her happy but she just couldn't seem to walk away. Everyone kept telling her she should do herself a favor and leave, but she wouldn't. We asked her, "What is it that makes you want to stay so much?" As unbelievable as it may seem, she would bring up times in the past of how nice he *used* to treat her and what nice things he *used* to do for her; and if only she could get him to be like that again, she just knew that they could be happy. We replied, "But what does he do *now* to make you feel like he values you?"

It was heartbreaking because she seemed to be stuck in a time warp. She always referred to how things *used* to be and how in love with her he was in the beginning and that he was just going through something and she just knew things would get better. It had been a year and a half since things were good with no relief in sight.

Just how much of her precious time was she willing to give him to change back to the person who respected her and loved her? As it turned out, she gave him another year, and not only did things not get better, they got worse. She finally recognized that she couldn't force him to change and realized she couldn't change anyone but herself.

It was very difficult for her, but she left him. Now, a year later, she looks back and in retrospect wonders how she could have stayed so long in a relationship where she did all the giving and he did all the taking. Hindsight is always 20/20.

So when you think he is so wonderful that you just can't leave him, yet you are unhappy, ask yourself, "Do his actions show me he values me?" If you are honest with yourself, you will probably be surprised by the answer.

Chapter Four

Use the
Double-Standard Method

Don't compromise yourself. You are all you've got.
                                    — Janis Joplin

THERE HAVE BEEN MANY TIMES IN MY RELATIONSHIPS
where I just couldn't think clearly. Trying to decide if certain of his
behaviors were acceptable or not became a lively debate in my mind;
perhaps I was being unfair or unreasonable. I thought that maybe I
shouldn't even say anything about how unhappy his behavior was
making me and how unfair I thought he was being. On the other hand,
maybe he actually *was* out of line, and I, without a doubt, had every
right to voice my opinion about the situation that was causing me pain.
I couldn't discern if I was out of line by saying something or if he was
out of line by treating me with less consideration than I believed was fair.

Of course, there would be times when I made the decision that I
was absolutely justified in saying something. I would then put my cards
on the table, and he would somehow turn it around and say I was being
unreasonable. He would go on to tell me how I just didn't understand

him, at which point I would begin to beat myself up for not being the good, understanding partner every man longs for. As I chastised myself, I began to have the same gnawing thoughts. Maybe it wasn't him, after all — maybe there was something wrong with the way I was acting.

Isn't it sad how little credit we give our intuition? A good indication that something is wrong in your relationship is when you aren't happy. You need to begin to recognize that it isn't all in your head and you aren't just making up his behavior. Something is going on in your life that is very real, and you have every right to look at it and confront it without feeling that you are the one who is at fault.

When you find yourself in the throes of a relationship, many times it is difficult to think with a level head and use your common sense. Since you are looking at your situation through your emotions, it is impossible to be objective. There are many ways in which we distort our thinking, and if we weren't mired so deeply in the relationship, our ability to rationalize fairly and realistically would be greatly enhanced.

For example, if you had a friend who was making excuses for some kind of unreasonable behavior that you would never tolerate in a relationship, you could objectively look at the situation and say, "What in God's name has gotten into you? Why do you allow this jerk to treat you like this?" Although you can see it clearly, your friend, being emotionally involved, unfortunately doesn't have your perspective.

My friend Lisa couldn't see straight when it came to Mr. Wonderful. So to help her see what everyone else saw I suggested that she write a personal ad describing the kind of man that she was stuck with in this relationship. It went something like this:

Wanted: Selfish and unaffectionate. Someone who loves to play golf on special occasions and doesn't show up for social events, so I can go alone. Cheap, inconsiderate, and indifferent. Make me pay for everything; I won't leave you. Throw me as few crumbs as possible just so I know I'm still alive. And I prefer someone who lies about where he is; it keeps my life exciting.

Another one of my hopelessly romantic friends was with a guy that no one liked. *Her* personal ad would have read something like this:

Wanted: Seeking a good-looking, well-dressed, seemingly successful con artist. Someone who will make me feel like I'm on top of the world while you steal my money. Cheaters, liars, and men obsessed with strip bars please respond. I like spending my nights wondering where you are, and other women's lipstick on your clothes won't make me leave you.

Why don't you try it yourself? Write your own personal ad describing the man in your life — and be honest with yourself. Is this the kind of person you would fix up with someone you cared about?

It is incredible to watch someone ignore all the signs and stay in a destructive relationship. Unless you have always had it together with very healthy boundaries in your relationships, my guess is that at one time or another you have experienced being the emotionally handicapped friend, or conversely, the dime store therapist (which any good friend naturally becomes to a friend in need).

In his *Feeling Good Handbook*, Dr. David Burns recommends different methods of untwisting your thinking. The Double Standard Method is my favorite because I personally believe I am good at giving what I think is great advice to my friends, but when it would come to my own situation, I was like a sinking ship.

It goes like this: What would you say to a close friend who was very much like you and had a similar relationship? Would you verbally beat her up saying things like…you're so stupid, this is all your fault… you'll never meet anyone again…you blew it…why didn't you say this or do that…or you should've been nicer or smarter or prettier or more subservient etc. etc. … Sound familiar?

Or would you be more supportive, a lot kinder, and more realistic? Be your own best friend! How can you be happy when you are constantly criticizing yourself? Don't be so hard on yourself and stop beating yourself up. Remember, it's not all your fault. It takes two to tango. You've got the steps down, the right outfit and tango music, but the wrong partner.

Lighten up on yourself. Pretend you're talking to your friend and she is crying on your shoulder with the same gory details. What would be your advice to her? Really listen to what you would say. Now…take your own advice.

Chapter Five

You Know You
Saw Red Flags

Certain signs precede certain events.
— *Cicero*

IN EVERY RELATIONSHIP THERE ARE TELLTALE SIGNS THAT give you some indication as to what kind of person you are getting involved with. Some of these signs are more obvious than others, but they are definitely there if you open your eyes and are honest with yourself.

I have a friend who was dating several men at the same time. One night we were at a Christmas party, and she and the host really hit it off. She hadn't met anyone she was actually attracted to in a long time, and she was excited because she had finally met someone she clicked with. He was successful and handsome and he even had a personality. They partied into the wee hours of the morning, and then she spent the night with him.

Yes — she absolutely broke Cardinal Rule #1 by sleeping with him. Of course, deep down inside she knew it, but she hoped against hope because they had such a great time together. Well, that was Saturday night, and he didn't call her until the following Sunday night. (He was "very busy" all week.) *Big Red Flag!*

She had a tortuous week, condemning herself for sleeping with him and wondering if he'd call. I told her that yes, she did make a mistake by sleeping with him — let it be a lesson learned. But *he* broke the *Unspoken rule of the world*: You never sleep with someone and not call the next day or at the very least the second day afterwards — unless, of course, you couldn't care less.

I tried to convince her that even though she had made a mistake, his was even more egregious and that she didn't want a man who obviously had so little respect for her. And if and when he *did* call, tell him as nicely as possible to hit the road. But did she listen? Of course not! She went out with him two more times. Evenings ending the same way — in bed — and the weeks between dates were as anxiety-filled as ever until…guess what happened? He just quit calling. Imagine that!

Well, if she had been honest with herself and not made excuses for his behavior, she would have saved herself a lot of self-flagellation, time, and worry. Even though her situation was somewhat extreme, it is an example of an obvious Red Flag she chose to ignore.

Not all Red Flags are so obvious. Some are more subtle. But you still need to get your Red Flag Detector out, dust it off, and use it. Quit making excuses for him — *you shouldn't have to*. Red Flags are warning signs of potential problems in the future.

Here are of some of the less obvious Red Flags:

- If he only sees you on weekdays.
- If he calls last minute to see you.
- If he spent a lot of time with you in the beginning, but now you're seeing less and less of him.
- You're always feeling like an afterthought or second choice.
- He tells you he loves you, but his actions don't prove it.
- There is always something wrong with you.
- He's always right…you're always wrong.
- His inability to compromise.

- You always find yourself crying or feeling bad.
- You can't communicate with him no matter how hard you try.
- His way is the only way.
- Your feelings don't matter.
- You are never perfect enough.
- He's a Mama's boy.
- Other peoples' feelings matter more than yours.
- He tries to change your personality.

And the list goes on and on....

Use these as warning signals. Slow down. Step back and re-evaluate: Is this really what I'm willing to tolerate from someone? This is another reason why it is so important for you to know yourself, so you can know if this is what you want in a mate.

Remember, we're not talking about someone's idiosyncrasies... everyone has their little quirks that drive us crazy. I'm talking about behavior that makes you feel unloved. The things you find yourself arguing with him about and find him consistently making excuses for — not just a late phone call here or there. We're discussing the blatant lack of consideration followed by an unnerving attitude of indifference. You know exactly what I'm talking about — the stuff that just plain makes you feel bad.

Don't waste your time with the wrong man. Use these Red Flags to your benefit so you can keep yourself available for when Mr. Right does come along.

Chapter Six

What Happened?
It Started Out So Good

*Although the world is full of suffering it is also full of
the overcoming of it.*

— Helen Keller

WHEN REFLECTING BACK ON OUR RELATIONSHIPS, WE HAVE
a tendency to focus only on the good in them. This is a point where
a lot of us get stuck. If he treated me so well before, he could treat me
that way again. It was great in the beginning; I just know he has it in
him. What happened? Well, what happened is this: He's got you where
he wants you; he's confident you're not going anywhere; and now the
real Mr. Wonderful emerges.

Everyone puts their best foot forward in the beginning, and later
they let their hair down; that's normal. You become more comfortable
with the person and trust them more, and while spending more time
together, you naturally see different sides of each other's personality.
Of course there are sides of everyone's personality that may grate on

your nerves, but that's tolerable; however, that's not what we are discussing here.

The beginning of all relationships is generally a romance made in heaven. I used to date a guy who would call me so much he would ask me if he was bothering me. At the time, I was falling for him and I loved the attention he was lavishing on me. He would buy me cute little cards for no reason just to show me how much he cared. He would send me flowers and tell me how special I was. He used to tell me that he wanted to have a relationship with more intimacy and openness than he had ever had before. He believed I was his soul-mate, and he knew without a doubt that he was going to marry me. We laughed a lot together. We would have what he called "rap sessions" just to hear what the other was thinking and feeling, not to mention that our sex life was incredible.

But all these things, little by little, became less and less. What happened to him? Where did he go? Was that ever really him? It started out so good...but everything changed. He changed. He wasn't remotely the same person. Eventually, after much agonizing and soul-searching, I decided to leave.

Believe me, it wasn't something I wanted to do, because I was still in love with him — or, more realistically, I was in love with who he used to be — but I knew what I had to do. I wanted the relationship to work more than anything, and I absolutely did not want to walk away, but I really didn't have a choice unless, of course, I wanted to stay in a relationship that was clearly not making me happy.

It wasn't the little nuances of his personality that I couldn't live with — I could accept those things. It was the downright disregard for my feelings and definite lack of mutual purpose in our relationship that drove me away. He really was no longer the person I had met. It wasn't the fact that the initial romancing had waned — that's to be expected. It was that once he had me where he wanted me, he turned into an inconsiderate, indifferent jerk.

We simply did not want the same things. I wanted to have a relationship and was willing to work at it, but he wasn't. It was very hard for me to leave, but I did so realizing that even though it was painful at that time, in time I would be okay. Sometimes even knowing that doesn't make it any easier to end it; you just know it is something you have to do. If you really listen to your intuition, you know when you should stay or go. Your intuition is there for a reason. It's your inner self, your soul communicating with you. Don't dismiss it — it can be your best friend.

Although every relationship has its ups and downs, the problems begin when the so-called "sides" of one's personality are abusive, neglectful, inconsiderate, or disrespectful on a *consistent* and *ongoing* basis. The difficulty lies in thinking you can change this behavior and control the situation.

This is generally when the struggle ensues. You try everything in your power to make him see your side, understand how you feel, change the way he thinks or acts, and try to make him realize that what he's doing or what he's not doing is ruining your relationship. But alas, you can't make someone love you. You cannot make someone do something they don't want to do. The only person you can control is yourself. You need to take back your power and change the direction in which your life is heading. You don't deserve to feel bad anymore.

Yes, I'm sure it *was* good in the beginning, but that person obviously was not the real person. The real person is what you have now. It's one thing for the honeymoon stage to be over, but it's another story when it's over and what you find is a totally different person.

Keep in mind that we have a tendency to remember only the good times. So whenever you play back the tape, play back the *whole* tape. What you see is reality. Aren't you glad you don't have to deal with it anymore? You deserve better and if you give yourself a chance, you'll find better.

Chapter Seven

He's Not the
Last Man on Earth

*Is there anyone so wise as to learn from the experience
of another?*

— Voltaire

I KNOW YOU THINK HE'S THE ONLY MAN IN THE WORLD.
I've heard it all before…I'll never meet anyone else…or…I'll never
love anyone like I loved him…or…I'll never have as much fun…
or…laugh as much…or…have as good sex…or…find anyone I can
talk to like I could talk to him…or who I had as much in common
with…that smelled as good…that liked the same foods…same music…
same movies…same sports, etc. I've heard it all.

Now look at it realistically: *Never say never.* This is totally irrational thinking that for some reason goes along with the first month or
two after the breakup. (For some it may be longer if you let it, but that's
your choice.) When you allow yourself to get beyond that first month
or two of irrational thinking, "never"…turns into…"yet." It may sound
something like this: Well, I haven't met anyone *yet* that I laugh with
as much or I haven't met anyone *yet* that I have as much fun with or
I just haven't met anyone *yet*.

The key word here is *YET* — which means that there is, without
a doubt, hope that there will be someone else, and *there will be*. It may
not happen as quickly as you'd like, but it *will* happen, and until then
you must have faith. You weren't looking for someone when you met

him. Wasn't there at least one other man in your life that you thought you couldn't live without? And isn't it amazing…you survived, got over him, and now you found another one that you can't live without. Be confident that you will get beyond this guy, too — and you *will* be all the better for it.

I can't begin to tell you how many times I've said the words, "I'll never meet anyone that I love like I loved him." In retrospect, it sounds ridiculous that anyone could be so narrow-minded. There were times that I believed I would never meet anyone, but the most amazing thing would inevitably happen: Not only would I find another man who I fell in love with, but every single time, the new relationship was better than the last. And in the most uncanny way, it was better in the exact area in which the last one was lacking. Eventually, I came to understand that there will always be life after whatever-his-name-is.

My friend Terri was beside herself after her breakup. Even I was beginning to think she wasn't going to pull through. She refused to believe that she could go on and have a great life. She simply would not let go of wanting the wrong man. I think the wake-up call came when she almost lost her job — a job she loved. She was forced to pull her head out of the sand, take a good look at what she was doing to her life, and make some very serious changes. She started going out with friends again and eventually met the man she was sure she would never meet.

Knowing you will meet someone doesn't always ease your pain, but it certainly gives you hope for a brighter future. Once the initial pain of the breakup starts to subside, you can be sure that there will be someone very special who will come into your life. It may take a little bit of time, but what's worth having is worth waiting for.

So believe it when I tell you that *YET* is a new beginning — it's the beginning of hope. Remember, there are a lot of men out there who want a good relationship. Men who are loving, honest, and able to commit — you just haven't met them *YET*!

Chapter Eight

Don't Make Excuses for the Way He Treats You

Is there a "cure" for a broken heart? Only time can heal your broken heart, just as only time can heal his broken arms and legs.

— Miss Piggy

SOMEWHERE ALONG THE LINE YOU DECIDED IT'S OKAY TO be treated, shall we say, less than desirably, and you put up with it, thinking, of course, that if you give him time or talk to him about it or give him space, his behavior will change. Hello-*ooooo*!

Zebras don't change their stripes.

Oh, sure, in the beginning it's different. They've got their best foot forward so they can get you where they want you — hooked — and then their true colors start to show. Which habits start to rear their ugly heads? Is it that he doesn't call when he says he will or that he just doesn't call, period?…Does he start criticizing the way you look, talk, or act? Or maybe you've made a wonderful dinner, and he walks in two hours late and somehow it's *your* fault. Do you complain too much about him taking sides with his ex-wife? Does he tell you he can't talk to his kids about how disrespectful they're acting toward you because they are going through a tough time and he doesn't want to upset them any more than they already are?

In fact, whatever he does wrong or disrespectful is incredibly transformed into "*your fault*." (Remember, these guys are rarely or never wrong.) Or perhaps he promises you that since he can't see you Friday, he'll see you Saturday, and he shows up at 10 P.M. wondering why you're so upset...or he promises to go on a vacation that never gets planned for one reason or another...etc. Promises, promises, promises — that always seem to get broken.

A friend of mine was dating a man who very shortly after they began seeing each other started showing signs of major inconsideration. Within the first month, after the novel bouquet of flowers and other expected niceties, he started playing golf both Saturday and Sunday from 11 A.M. to 7 or 8 P.M. And if that wasn't bad enough, whenever he did come over to see her, he was really tired and wanted to go to sleep. Wow! Wasn't he a blast to be around? And doesn't that usually happen after about 5 or 10 years of marriage, if at all?

No one could believe that after one month he was already acting as if he preferred the company of his friends over being with her. I'm not suggesting that couples shouldn't have separate interests; as a matter of fact, I would encourage it because it's healthy. But I believe this to be a blatant lack of compromise on his part. Not only did he work late all week (getting home between 8 and 10 P.M.), but she also rarely saw him on weekends. What kind of relationship is that — the 10 P.M. to 7 A.M. kind?

To celebrate her birthday he was going to take her out for a fabulous dinner to her favorite restaurant. She was all dressed up in her sexy black dress, makeup on, hair looking great, and ready at 6 P.M., just as they had planned. She waited and waited, but he didn't show up until 8:00 P.M. Not only did he show up late without even the courtesy of a phone call, he then proceeded to inform her that it wasn't going to be just the two of them going out for her birthday dinner. He had invited some friends, and further, she should change into something more casual because they were going to the local pub. To add insult to injury, before they even left the house, he told her that he was really tired and whenever they came home, he just wanted to go to sleep. No birthday sex for her! *Big Red Flag!*

The most unbelievable part of all of this is that she made excuses for him, put up with it, and therefore never got her needs met. I tried to explain to her that by accepting this kind of behavior, she was only setting herself up for more of the same. She couldn't grasp the concept "*We teach people how to treat us.*" I urged her to speak up about the unfairness of the situation and try to discuss some kind of a compromise, but the reason she didn't want to was that she was afraid if she said something she would lose him. What a loss!

I know that accepting this kind of treatment may seem hard to fathom for some people, but when you have low self-esteem, this is how you allow yourself to be treated. Living with low self-esteem makes it difficult to set boundaries, and your own needs take a back seat to what's-his-names'. If you don't like it, then stop doing it to yourself. Rid yourself of the chains that keep you imprisoned in painful relationships.

Broken promises, missed phone calls, forgotten birthdays, and lonely weekends…why do you allow yourself to be treated like that? And why on earth do you make excuses for him? There is absolutely no excuse for the *non*-consideration of your time, your feelings, or your commitment. What is the excuse for having no regard for your feelings? You deserve *so* much better. Let go of this jerk. Trust me, you will get over him in time, and you'll thank God that you did.

The lesson here is to open your eyes and read the signs. If you always seem to be upset and sad, there is a reason — don't kid yourself…*actions really do speak louder than words*. If he's not treating you the way you want to be treated, and he makes excuses for it, run in the other direction. When you get to where you want to be, you'll be glad you did.

_____Chapter Nine_____

Holding On To Hope

*There is not enough darkness in all the world to put out
the light of even one small candle.*

— *Robert Alden*

ONE NIGHT, MY GIRLFRIEND AND I WERE DISCUSSING RELA-
tionships. She asked me why I thought she was having such a difficult
time telling her former boyfriend not to call her anymore. The relationship was over, but she was struggling with letting go, and occasion-
ally, he would call just to see how she was doing. Or maybe he was
calling to dangle the proverbial carrot to keep her hanging on — just
in case. Every time he called, it stirred in her the hope that there might
be a chance things really could work out.

We were throwing around different possibilities as to why she might
be having a tough time telling him to stop calling her. She wanted to
get on with her life, and his attempts to keep the flame lit were only
prolonging her agony. She thought that generally women don't just
come out and say, "Don't call me anymore" because they hold on to
the fantasy that the man will finally realize what he lost and come back,
therefore restoring and affirming their worth.

She said, "We should come up with a name for this, a term." And I said, "There already is a term...stupidity!" Although it was funny at the time, the sad truth is that some hold on to hope longer than they should. This "holding on syndrome" is sometimes contributed to a certain kind of wishful thinking. Some of your thoughts may be

- If he misses you enough, he'll realize how much you meant to him, and he will come running back.
- You love him so much, and through some kind of telepathy, it will hit him, and he'll come back.
- He'll come back for the sake of the kids.
- If you give him enough time, he will change.
- Somehow you know that, deep down inside, he really loves you, and you just know he'll come back.

There are a number of reasons why we hold on to hope. We don't want to start over, either. That conjures up a whole array of reasons why we'd rather stay with the old, the bad, and the familiar: the dating scene (not again) or blind dates (*never* again!); worrying about AIDS and other sex-related issues and the awkwardness of addressing them; getting to know someone else's family; and the risk of being hurt again. Well, you don't have to risk being hurt again if you stay in a bad relationship, because there is no risk at all — you can be 100% sure you will get hurt again. So you would have better odds with someone new.

Anyway, holding on to hope is the last step in letting go. You've invested a lot of time, energy, and emotion in this relationship, and it's difficult to let go of something you've worked hard nurturing and that you so desperately want to save. It's not easy to let go of your dreams, and we naturally hold out hope for something we want so deeply.

But all the wishing, dreaming, and hoping are not going to change the fact that you are in an unhealthy relationship, and the one thing you need to do most is admit to yourself that it's over...and let go. This can be the hardest step for some people because it makes it so final. You finally realize your plans with this person will never come true, and that's a bitter pill to swallow.

The key here is to remember your hopes and dreams are still very much real, but it's the person that will change in fulfilling these dreams. You wouldn't want a daughter, niece, or friend to try and fulfill her dreams with someone who didn't treat her with love, consideration, and respect. In that case, she would only have attained her desire to be *in* a relationship — but not in the *kind* of relationship she had always dreamed of for herself — the kind she deserves.

The good news is that by letting go of the past, you now have the opportunity to start over. Now you have a chance to really make your dreams come true — *that* is the hope you should hold on to. So when you start to hold on to the hope of him coming back a new and improved man (that's really dreaming) and the two of you sailing off into the sunset, refocus your hope to finding a man with whom you have a chance of having a fulfilling, healthy relationship. Give yourself a chance: Let go of the past...and you *will* have a better future. If you begin your inward journey and discover the reasons you stay in these kinds of relationships, you will also be able to let go of the self-defeating behaviors that cause you to continue to repeat the same pattern.

There are many examples of women who held on to the hope that the abusive men they were in love with would somehow change. Mind you, the level of abuse ranges from repeated inconsideration and disrespect all the way to emotional and even physical abuse. One well-known example is the relationship between O. J. Simpson and Nicole Brown. She kept leaving and coming back, believing he might change, but he never did. Of course, we all know the sad outcome.

Another example is of a friend of mine who was in a relationship with a man who continually cheated on her, each time promising her it was the last. She continued to go back hoping things would be different, and they never were. She wasted seven years of her life in a very destructive relationship before she finally let go. She is now married to a wonderful man.

In each of the above examples, it's the false hope these women held on to that kept them trapped. We all want to love and be loved. Unfortunately, this isn't always a two-way street. When you are in a relationship, and it's good, you know it — but when it's *not* good, you know it too.

So remember: When you hold on to hope, you simply postpone the inevitable. Stop wasting your time. If he hasn't changed yet, don't make the mistake of thinking if you go back things will change. He may change for a short time but chances are very good that all the hoping in the world isn't going to make it happen.

Chapter Ten

What Is Your Excuse for Staying in an Unhappy Relationship...and Don't Say "Because I Love Him"

*Destiny is not a matter of chance, it is a matter of
choice; it is not a thing to be waited for, it is a thing to
be achieved.*

— *William Jennings Bryan*

SOMETIMES, LOVE JUST ISN'T ENOUGH. SAD...BUT TRUE.
Remember growing up when you believed in the fantasy that everyone
lived happily ever after? That love conquers all? Well, guess what? *This*
is reality.

I'm not suggesting you can't live your life and have your dreams
fulfilled; you should aspire to reach your dreams. But reality sets in when
you are trying to fulfill your dreams with someone and he isn't even
aware of what your dreams *are* — or maybe even if he was aware, he
wouldn't care.

This person you think you want in your life is on a different path, the wrong page, has another agenda. He doesn't even have a clue what you are talking about (of course, to him, you are always nagging) or he doesn't care what you are talking about. He doesn't listen, he doesn't want to hear it, "it's all your fault," and "there you go again."

A relationship is between *two* people, interacting, communicating their feelings, compromising, sharing and building their dreams *together* — the key word being *together*. Then and only then can you make your mutual dreams come true. It's impossible to have a great relationship with someone else...all by yourself. You have to relate somehow with the other person.

If you are married or living together and you are not connecting in any way, shape, or form outside of the bedroom, you don't have a relationship with this person — you have a living arrangement. If you're not living together and you're in a relationship where you're not communicating or relating on any level, you carry a lot of heartache and pain. But for some reason, you think you should be together, even if all of the signs point to the opposite. Maybe you've even kidded yourself into believing you were meant to be together.

There are a number of reasons people rationalize staying in bad relationships. Below are some of the excuses I hear most often:

> *"We've been together for so long,*
> *I've invested so much time."*

All the more reason not to waste another precious second! Even with all the time you have been together, you still can't make it work; what makes you think you can make it work now?

> *"The children...I'm staying for them."*

I love this one. Parents are the most powerful role models for their children. Children learn how to have a relationship from observing the adults in the house and the way they interact. In essence, you are teaching your son or daughter both how to be treated in a relationship and how to treat someone. If you are being abused in any large or small sense of the word and you stay, do you think that perhaps the message you are sending is, 'It's okay to be treated like this and you should just accept it'? On the other hand, what they may be learning is, 'This is how you treat someone and you can do whatever you want without any regard for the other person. There are no repercussions, and they will come back for more.' And please don't act as if your children don't see what's going on — give them some credit. No matter what their age, they sense the truth of their environment. I can't imagine that this is the kind of life you would want your children to choose for themselves...to be abused or be an abuser. By *not* teaching them *by example* how to have healthy boundaries, you are significantly raising their chances of ending up in a relationship similar to yours.

"Where would I go...I don't have any money?"

If there is a will, there is a way. Easier said than done, but true. There are a lot of ways to find and get employment and a roof over your head. It may not be "The Ritz" at first, but it's something to work toward. This will be *your* home, filled with all the things you want and the promise of a new beginning and a brighter future. Look around; people are making money every day. The hardest thing to do is... *take the first step.* If you want it badly enough, you will find a way to make it happen. Don't use this as an excuse for not starting a new life. The alternative is more of what you already have, and you wouldn't be reading this book if you haven't had just about enough. So *believe in yourself. Search for the strength — it's there.* You will be surprised by what you are capable of doing.

"I'll never love anyone like I love him."

This is an easy one. As I've said before, I'm sure there have been men in your past you thought you just couldn't live without. As far as "never" meeting anyone else, unless you are a hermit or a monk, it's almost impossible to live on this earth without running into people. You do grocery shop, don't you? I'm sure I've seen you at the gas station filling your car. When you least expect it, there he is. Of course, now all you have to do is be open to meeting someone new, because believe me, it will happen. (Let's pray that you're doing your homework and learning to like yourself, so when you enter the next relationship it will be a healthy one.)

I told you not to say it, but I knew you would ...

"Because I love him!"

I believe that you do love him. That's not the problem. The problem is — you're not being loved back the way you want to be. Loving someone and not being loved back is not a relationship — it's a one-way street. I'm sure he's got his good points. But if *your* needs are not being met, no amount of loving him is going to fill that empty space. You can love him all you want but if it's not mutual, who needs it? Why would you want it?

If you've been together for any significant length of time and are still clearly not happy, you are probably not getting the love you want or deserve. *Don't settle for less.* Give yourself a second chance. Find someone who is on the same page, walking down the same path. Find someone who *wants* to love you...not someone that you have to *get* to love you.

There are plenty of men out there who are capable of having and who want to have a happy relationship. Quit making excuses and wasting your time! The sooner you can do that, the sooner you can find a person with whom you will live happily and healthily ever after.

Chapter Eleven

Maybe You Miss Having a Man in Your Life... But It's Not Worth Having the Wrong One

It's not easy to find happiness in ourselves, and it is not possible to find it elsewhere.

— Agnes Repplier

I KNOW IT'S HARD. YOU'RE USED TO HAVING SOMEONE around...someone to talk to...to go to the movies with...to rent movies...to go to dinner...to just do nothing with, etc. But I bet you don't miss the criticism, the verbal abuse, the physical abuse, the lack of consideration for your feelings, the obvious lack of respect for you, the rudeness, the indifference, the blame, the selfishness, or whatever your personal circumstance. You don't miss the things that made you want to leave in the first place.

When I ended my last relationship, I knew it was the right thing to do because I was not getting many of my needs met. Plus, according to my friends, I was very unhappy. Even though there were times I didn't want to admit it, the truth is that most of the time I was very unhappy. Although I knew leaving was the best thing for me, I really didn't want to do it because I didn't want to start all over again. I wanted to avoid going through everything that goes along with "The Breakup."

I liken it to going through withdrawal — similar to breaking a bad habit, such as smoking. You know you should quit because 'it's so bad for you,' so you give it up. And it seems that the first few weeks or months, it's the only thing you can think about; you want it so badly. And even though you know it isn't healthy, you still want it. It's an *addiction*.

This was always the hard part for me to understand. I left because I wasn't happy, yet I missed being with someone who wasn't being fair to me. Why? I came to realize that although his feelings may have changed, I couldn't turn my feelings on and off like a faucet. I still had strong feelings for this person, and it would take some time for me to let go. Yes, I missed him — that's normal. But it became increasingly clear that what I missed was the person he was in the beginning, someone who didn't exist in reality anymore but only in my hopeful imagination. I certainly didn't miss how he had treated me — I missed how I thought he *could* treat me, but rarely did. It was as if what I actually missed was my fantasy of who I wanted him to be, but it was obvious that what I really wanted, he was definitely not providing.

Hopefully, in this situation you come to the only conclusion that will help keep your sanity — you walk away! Now you must begin the healing process, which will enable you to be open to meeting someone new — someone who wants the same things you do, like a good relationship.

I worked with a girl named Stephanie. To put it mildly, she was being treated like crap, but she continued to stay with this guy. She kept saying, "He's better than no one at all." Or, "Better the evil that I know than one I don't know." All she wanted was to be in a relationship. It obviously didn't matter who it was with, because no one would actually go out and pick a jerk like this and want to stay with him. Lucky for him, she had a warped attitude about relationships. She continued to cater to his needs, ignore his lies, deny that he was cheating, and to always put herself last. Why? For several reasons: her self-esteem issues, not believing she deserved more, and she was afraid to be alone, to name a few.

It's nice having someone around, but it's not worth having someone around if he doesn't treat you the way you want to be treated or doesn't fulfill your needs. You don't miss him (okay, you probably miss certain parts of him) but what you *do* miss is companionship, love, and just having someone else around. That's the key here, having *someone* around, not necessarily having *him* around. In reality, you don't miss him as much as you miss "someone."

In time, there will be someone, and it will be a healthier, more rewarding relationship because you will be smarter and stronger.

So remember, the next time you feel you miss having someone to go to the movies with or to go to dinner with…go with your friends because they're someone, too, you know — and *they'll* treat you right. In time, you'll find that special someone you love having around.

Part Two

MOVING ON

Chapter Twelve

Go Through the Stages; You Will Get Beyond Them

God give us the grace to accept with serenity the things that cannot be changed, courage to change the things which should be changed, and the wisdom to distinguish the one from the other.

— Reinhold Niebuhr

WHEN YOU END A RELATIONSHIP, IT CAN FEEL SO BAD THAT there are times you wonder how you are going to face another day. It may seem to go on for so long that you begin to think this feeling will never pass. It's the first thing on your mind when you wake up, and it's the last thought before you go to sleep — and it probably consumes a lot of your time in between.

Oh, it hurts all right. It's devastating. You wonder how you are even functioning at work without becoming a blubbering wreck (and sometimes you do), because as soon as you walk through your front door you break down — if you've even made it that far without falling apart in the car on your way home.

It feels as if your heart is actually breaking. You cannot believe this is really happening. You just know he is going to call...but he doesn't. (Hopefully for your sake he won't call, because at this point you might be weak enough to take him back, and as hard as it is, that would be the wrong thing to do.)

You're hurting so much that you start wondering if breaking up is the right thing to do. (Don't forget: You wouldn't have broken it off if you didn't have a good reason. It's not like you wanted it to end. You probably ended it because you tried everything short of absolute submission but nothing worked.) There's a part of you that honestly believes you'll never get over this feeling…but rest assured you will survive this pain if you let yourself.

When experiencing the loss of someone you love, there are stages that you will go through. They may vary in time and intensity, but you will inevitably suffer through each of them.

These stages are

- Shock. Disbelief. Denial.
- Fear. Anger. Depression.
- Understanding. Acceptance. Letting go.

At first, it may seem incomprehensible that he is really gone. You just don't want to believe that it's over. Even if you ended the relationship, you might play games with yourself by believing everything will somehow work out — that this is temporary, and you will be back together again someday.

That someday may come when you will try again and find yourself right back where you started when you ended it in the first place. It's hard to accept something that you really didn't want to happen, but alas, the healing will only begin when you finally start to accept the fact that *it really is over*.

You may also begin to feel depressed because you are lonely. You're afraid you won't meet anyone that you could feel the same way about, and you're angry because you spent so much of your precious time trying to make a bad relationship good. You may cry a lot because your hopes for a life together with this person are destroyed.

Allow yourself to grieve. It's normal. Get it out so you can let it go. As time passes you will begin to realize that all your tears won't bring him back.

It's unfortunate, but at this stage you may still think you want him back. If you allow yourself the luxury of getting over this guy, someday you will look back and say, "It makes me sick to think about how much time I wasted in that relationship, and now when I think back to how long it took me to stop crying over him, I can't believe it myself!"

Eventually, you will accept that he is gone, and it is time for you to move on. In time, you will get over him, and hopefully, you will even understand it worked out for the best! I can't tell you how many people I've talked to while writing this book who commented on the fact that if they had stayed instead of leaving, they can say without a doubt they would have had a miserable life. Most of them said, "You couldn't pay me to go back there now."

So while you are still having fleeting thoughts of what you shared together, keep in mind those thoughts will eventually become fewer and fewer. It's in letting go of the past that you can start to live in the present and begin to build a future.

Take comfort in knowing that the feelings you are experiencing are merely a phase that you will overcome in time. These stages are part of a very normal passage that will lead you to life after whatever-his-name-is. Remember, nothing lasts forever, not even this feeling. Hold on to the promise that time does heal all wounds. Trust that this is a process...and you *will* survive.

Take time to read self-help books that capture your interest...rely on good friends...stay positive and stay busy. This is a time when you really have to monitor your thoughts. When you slip into negative thinking, immediately turn your thoughts to what it is you desire. Focus on what you want, not on what you don't want. Your life is a direct reflection of the kind of thoughts that dominate your mind. If you take control of your thoughts, you will single-handedly change your life experiences. Even if you can't believe it's possible now, eventually you will see the truth. With every door that closes, another one opens.

There is life after whatever-his-name-is, and if *you* believe it, it will be a good life. This is a time of growth for you and hopefully someday you will look back and say, "Thank God I got out of that relationship."

Remember — what you are going through is a natural stage that you will get beyond. Trust yourself! You walked away from him for a reason. Take it one day at a time. Be patient and strong. You will be a better person for it.

Chapter Thirteen

Don't Second-Guess Yourself

Just trust yourself, then you will know how to live.
— *Goethe*

OKAY, NOW THINK ABOUT IT: IT'S NOT LIKE YOU WOKE UP one day and said, "He treats me so damn well, I think I'll end it"…or "We have such a great relationship — I'm going to dump him." If you would just leave, that would be great, but my guess is that you're struggling with letting go, and that's why you're reading this book.

Don't second-guess yourself! Use pain as a warning sign that something is wrong. Obviously, there is some good reason that you've considered walking away from the months or years of your life that you have already invested in this person. I'm sure there has been a lot of time, energy, and emotion that you've put into trying to make this work. So why, after all this effort, would you throw in the hat for no reason? You're possibly telling yourself, "Oh, what if I'm making a mistake?" or "Maybe it really wasn't that bad. I'm just blowing this out of proportion."

The only mistake you're making is even considering going back to a time-tested bad relationship, and the only thing that you're blowing out of proportion is that you think you've made a mistake. Go with your intuition. Listen to what your gut is telling you. Trust yourself. If you've gotten this far, you did so for a reason.

You do want a relationship, and you still love him or you *think* you love him; that's why it's so hard to walk away. But remember one important fact: You want a relationship with a man who respects and loves you — and if you give yourself time, that is what you will find.

The penalty you pay when you don't trust your instinct is a loss of valuable time. I was once in a relationship with a man that I thought was my soul-mate. He entered my life and literally swept me off of my feet. I was thirty-eight years old and had never been treated in such a romantic, thoughtful way. I traveled a lot for my job and whenever I would arrive at the front desk to check into my hotel, there would already be a sweet little message from Mr. Wonderful. He would be my early morning wake-up call, even though he didn't have to get up early.

He would always have a special card for me. He couldn't compliment me enough. He used to say the things that every woman longs to hear. I would call him my soap opera star because it was so great between us. It really was a very easy relationship, just as if we were meant to be together. We were compatible in many ways. There was no doubt we were head over heels in love.

Because we both traveled so much, we would rendezvous in different cities. With the end of summer approaching, he was now ending his extensive traveling schedule. He hadn't been home in the four months that I knew him, and we were both looking forward to spending time together on a more normal basis.

Everything was going great between us until he came home; that's when everything changed. He was nice, but not that nice, and he was different, very different. Of course, according to him, it was all in my imagination. He just wanted to spend time with his friends — and more time, and more time, until that's pretty much all he was doing. Needless to say, I was not only extremely disappointed, but I was also very hurt.

I put up with it, making excuses for the next two months, when I finally said enough is enough. I didn't want to put up with it anymore because I didn't deserve it. So I made the next logical move — I ended it. I actually felt good about it, because I knew I was doing the right thing for myself.

In the past, I would have stayed, made more excuses, and wondered why I was so miserable. But I had learned a valuable lesson from my past. I wasn't going to waste *my time* in another unfulfilling relationship. He wasn't worth it.

About a week later, a friend of mine called and asked how everything was going. I told him I had left and why I left. His response was not what I expected. He said I was making the biggest mistake of my life and that as far as he could see we were perfect together and I should call my ex and try to work things out.

Well, guess what? I listened to him instead of trusting myself, and that turned out to be the bigger mistake. This is a real-life classic example of second-guessing yourself. It was the wrong thing for me to do. I wasted another year of my life by not trusting myself and listening to *my* gut feeling.

So when you begin to question whether or not you are making a mistake by ending it, *trust your instincts.* Follow your feelings; it's when you ignore them that you get into trouble. Don't let anyone else influence the direction in which you should take your life. They are not you. After you have allowed them to make your decision for you, *you* will have to live with it. Who better to tell you what you want for your life than — you…imagine that!

You know in your heart when you are making the right or wrong decision for yourself. Having faith in your intuition and believing in yourself will make second-guessing yourself a thing of the past.

Chapter Fourteen

It's Natural to Go Through the Pain — Just Give Yourself Time

*If you are distressed by anything external, the pain is
not due to the thing itself, but to your estimate of it; and
this you have the power to revoke at any moment.*
                                        — *Marcus Aurelius*

ANY LOSS IS PAINFUL, WHETHER YOU WANTED IT, HE WANT-
ed it, or it was mutual. Even when you lose something small like an
earring or a watch, you feel bad. If you were to lose your job, you
would feel thrown into a situation that comes with a gamut of emotions, which are generally not all good. But when you lose your com-
panion, your lover, your best friend (or so you think), you lose your
hopes with that person, your dreams of what could have been. Some
may even lose a little self-esteem, and with that loss, there's a lot of
pain. There is no way around it...*pain is inevitable*; it's one of the main
reasons why people stay in relationships that aren't going so great.

We stay because we want to avoid the pain. Most of us probably
know from past experience that it hurts, and being human we try to

avoid hurt and pain at all costs, which usually means we stay when we know we should leave.

There were many opportunities for me to walk away from an on-again-off-again seven-year relationship, but for some reason, I didn't. I seemed to always keep myself right where I was...stuck in an emotionally unfulfilling relationship. Instead of dealing with the pain of the breakup and getting beyond it, I would conveniently rationalize away his indiscretions and think that somehow, by staying, I could handle the short-term pain more easily than the dramatic, long-term pain that goes along with breaking up. In the back of my mind, I just didn't feel strong enough to deal with the trauma and heartache that are inevitable with the demise of a relationship.

There comes a point when remaining in an unhealthy relationship becomes more painful than the actual pain of the breakup, and thus begins the hard part — taking the first step to walk away — and also the healing. The process takes time and, unfortunately, it is painful, but if you allow yourself the time to heal, life will get better.

I have a friend who was in a very emotionally abusive relationship for five years. Her boyfriend would constantly criticize the way she talked, dressed, and acted. If she gained even 5 pounds on her 5'6", 115-lb. body, he would tell her she didn't look sexy. Nothing she did was ever good enough...and she stayed. She would complain about him all the time...but she stayed.

When I asked her why she just didn't leave when it was obvious she was unhappy, she made a very interesting comment. She said, "I know I should leave but I'm just not ready to go through the pain of breaking up." I tried to convince her that even though it would be painful for the first five months or so (this healing time varies for everyone), that in five months, she would be that much further ahead in her healing process. But if she chose to stay, in five months she would still be in a relationship that was making her miserable. At least if she dealt with the pain now, she could be five months ahead of the program instead of simply delaying the inevitable.

She lasted two more years living in an emotionally unfulfilling relationship in hopes that things would get better. She stayed so she could avoid the pain that goes along with ending a relationship. The irony is she eventually had to go through it anyway. After much agonizing, she finally made the decision to leave, and when she looks back on it now, she is amazed that she didn't leave sooner.

I'm not suggesting you shouldn't try to work things out when you can. Communicating, compromising, and resolving differences are essential to making a relationship work. That's not what we are discussing here. We're talking about "The End," after you've already tried everything you can possibly think of to make it work. You've done all of the crying, talking, therapy, rationalizing, wishing, dreaming, screaming — everything short of doing somersaults naked down Main Street.

You know deep in your heart that you can't go on like this anymore — that it has to end.

The end signifies change, and change is uncomfortable and scary. You know that without a doubt this is going to cause you some pain… but "time heals all wounds" and in time you *will* get over this. You *will* feel better (if you let yourself). You *will* pick up the pieces and, as time passes, you *will* begin to realize that there is a better future for you.

So take it easy…take it a day at a time. Go through the pain. It's normal, and you will survive — and in the end, you'll be a better person for it.

Chapter Fifteen

Don't Be So
Hard on Yourself

*You have no idea what a poor opinion I have of myself
and how little I deserve it.*

— *W. S. Gilbert*

IT'S VERY DAMAGING TO YOUR SELF-ESTEEM WHEN YOU
continually blame yourself. Isn't it interesting that while you were *in*
the relationship everything was his fault, but now that it's over, everything is *your* fault. There is never only one person to blame: It always
has taken two to make or break it; it still *does* take two; and it always
will take two.

Once, when I ended a relationship with my boyfriend, for some
crazy reason I believed if only I had done things differently the outcome
would have been what I desired. I used to beat *myself* up for not being
more understanding when he would consistently show up late. Isn't that
ridiculous? He was the one who was inconsiderate, and I was the one
taking the blame. He would question why I was putting pressure on
him to make a commitment after we had been together for four years.
After all, he thought he should be the one to bring it up, not me. How
convenient — for *him*! Plus maybe if I had not been so insecure after
he cheated on me, he would have been more attracted to me; and let's

not forget, if I would have just lost 10 lbs., he would definitely have been more sexually attracted to me.

Looking back on it now, it's hard to believe I had such low self-esteem that I would allow myself to stay in such a demeaning relationship. The worst part was I would inconceivably blame myself. It is amazing what you will put up with when you don't value yourself. *That is why I can't emphasize enough to you how important it is to get to know and love yourself.* It takes a lot of work, but in the end you can look back and know that you will never allow yourself to be treated so miserably again, because you are worth so much more.

When you begin to beat yourself over the head about all the things you might have done differently, stop yourself and think about how *he* could have done things differently. Never forget you were not alone in this relationship. It's imperative that you look at how you contributed to the fall of your relationship and learn from it. There are some very important lessons to be learned, and if you don't learn them now, you will probably see them again.

My guess is that you probably treated him decently. That wasn't where you failed. The mistake was when you weren't being treated the way you deserved to be, and you actually stayed. You put up with it, and therein lies the mistake.

Now you know that when there are signs of any kind of mistreatment on a *consistent* basis, you can say "Sayonara" without second-guessing yourself. You don't deserve to be treated poorly, and I hope you finally realize it. Sure, there are things you could've done differently, but what good does it do to put yourself down? Can you change the past? No, but now you can use this knowledge to help you to avoid making the same mistakes again.

Does it help you feel better to go over and over what could've been? No! So why torture yourself? *Learn the valuable lessons that need to be learned.* Don't let this pain be for naught. You had to go through it; you might as well gain something from it. The hardest lessons in life are sometimes the most painful. It's normal to feel what you're feeling; just don't let it consume you in a negative way. It's your choice; *you* create what your life looks like.

You may not be able to see the light at the end of the tunnel yet, but it is definitely there waiting for you to arrive — and you will arrive. You have *so* much to look forward to: a brighter, richer future and a healthier and happier relationship.

Once you stop being so hard on yourself, every day you'll feel a little bit better. So focus on the goodness in your life. Say daily affirmations and keep the faith.

There really is life after what's-his-name.

Chapter Sixteen

Your Hand Should Fall Off Your Body Before You Pick Up the Phone to Call Him

*Experience enables you to recognize a mistake when
you make it again.*

— *Franklin P. Jones*

THIS IS A MISTAKE THAT I HAVE SEEN MANY OF MY FRIENDS make but one I can gratefully say that I haven't made more than once, thanks to my mother's advice. She would preach over and over again, "What ever you do, do NOT pick up that phone to call him. Call anyone but him. Just DON'T call him."

Of course, like most people I had to learn the first time the hard way. After breaking up with someone, it's only natural to want to talk to him for a few reasons. He's someone you are used to talking to frequently, kind of like a habit you now have to break. Or you might like to rehash some of the past and have a better understanding of why things happened the way they did. Besides, it is difficult to turn your feelings on and off like a faucet, you probably still love this person, and it's hard to let go.

So you let a little bit of time go by, and you just can't believe he hasn't called; you are *dying* to talk to him. You let a little more time go by, and now it's really driving you crazy and you just have to talk to him. So…you call.

What happened? Not only did he *not* tell you what you wanted to hear, but he seemed so…cold. How could he act so cool after all you have been through together? To add insult to injury, you almost got into another fight just like before. Imagine that! The question is, Do you feel better or worse now that you gave in and called? My experience and that of my friends says, unquestionably, it made us feel worse. Why?

There are a couple of reasons why you never, under any circumstances, pick up that phone to call him — whether or not you broke up with him, but particularly if he broke up with you. (Keep in mind this relationship was not fulfilling, and you were or are getting the short end of the stick.)

First of all, consider your pride. Don't give him the satisfaction of letting him think for one second that you're thinking of him (he already thinks that) or that you miss him (he thinks that too) — and by *not* calling, you keep your dignity and you also keep him wondering. Why feed into his already enlarged male ego? Don't give him the pleasure of thinking, "See, I knew she'd call," or "See, she can't stand being without me," or "I knew I was good — she really misses me." He's expecting you to call…all the more reason *not* to call.

Secondly, it's over. You have nothing to talk about. Do you want to tell him how much he hurt you? Haven't you told him a hundred times already? He knows how much he hurt you and obviously didn't care enough to stop it. If he acts like he doesn't know how much he hurt you, then he's an idiot. Some men like to conveniently play stupid. Remember, there's nothing you can say that is going to change what happened or change him, so save your time, your emotions, and your breath.

My friend Sara broke up with her boyfriend, and she couldn't believe he didn't call her. He was the one that ruined their relationship by cheating on her, and of course she thought he was going to call to make things right. She couldn't stand it anymore. So, guess what? She called him. The question is, Why would she want to — what was she trying to accomplish? Hopefully not to get back together! She made some lame excuse as to why she was calling and not only did he *not* tell her what she wanted to hear but they got into huge fight. She was even more miserable after the call, because he was clearly not there for her. It just isn't worth it unless you actually love torturing yourself.

There's one thing calling him will do: make you feel worse and him feel better. And it will open up a can of worms that would be better left unopened. Or worse yet, it might cause you to go back to a relationship that you've already determined is bad for you, and you think for some unfathomable reason, after all you've done to try and make it work, that it will now get better. You will only be wasting more of your precious time to find out that in the end it will still be the same outcome.

Remember, this book isn't about reconciling. It's about breaking it off with Mr. Wrong and moving forward. So when you feel like calling him, call someone else, call anyone else…but please what ever you do…DON'T CALL HIM!

Chapter Seventeen

You Can Go Back With Him, But...

Facts do not cease to exist because they are ignored.
— *Aldous Huxley*

I HAVE SEEN THIS CYCLE REPEATEDLY WITH MY FRIENDS, myself, and a lot of the people with whom I've discussed relationships. You're in a relationship; you're unhappy; you've had enough; and finally you decide, after much agonizing, to end it. You actually get up the courage and walk away, and Mr. Who-Cares is totally shocked and amazed. He desperately wants you back, and he will do anything to get you back.

Whatever the circumstances, there generally seems to be an interesting twist in Mr. Who-Cares's actions, feelings, behavior, and overall attitude when you tell him it's over. He's suddenly enlightened to exactly what he did wrong. Even more interesting, he can finally feel your pain, understand everything you've been saying all of these past weeks, months, and years, and — even better — *now* he wants to make it up to you. He's going to change, because he doesn't want to lose you and he finally sees what a jerk he's been.

If you are really lucky, he will change, but that's like winning the lottery. Some men actually do see the light and with a strong resolve and true intention, they can effect a real change in themselves. So now that he's saying what you've always wanted to hear and you've been duped into thinking that he has changed, you decide to give him another chance. After all, you really do love him, and you are thrilled that he finally understands.

At first it's wonderful. It's everything you've always wanted it to be. He's doing things and saying things that he hasn't said or done for a long time. Usually, he will change for a very short period, but inevitably you will begin to see a lot of the old, the bad, and the ugly creeping back into your relationship again. Not only are you faced with the same old stuff, but now his attitude comes topped with a little bitterness and resentment for putting him through the torture he had to endure — namely, pretending to be nice.

One couple I know had been married for twenty years. From an outsider's view, their relationship looked just fine; they were attractive, financially comfortable, and had great kids. They had their ups and downs like all relationships, but behind closed doors, he shut her out. When he was angry about something, he wouldn't talk to her, have sex with her, or acknowledge that she was alive, and this was repeated year after year. After the pleas to stop shutting her out fell on deaf ears, my friend had had enough. She didn't know where else to turn. She begged him to go to counseling to no avail. She asked him over and over again to please hear what she was saying, which was usually accompanied by weeks of total silence. There was no communication whatsoever on his side. She cried a lot, and as the years went on she continually tried to get him to open up, and he never would.

Eventually her perseverance had worn thin — their relationship was damaged, and she couldn't handle much more rejection. Instead of ending it and walking away, she ended up turning to someone who would listen and found herself in the arms of another man. Of course her husband found out, and he was devastated. He now realized that there really was a problem, and he wanted to do anything he could in order not to lose his precious wife that he had taken for granted for all these years. He was now miraculously aware of all the wrongs he had done to their relationship, and he wanted desperately to right them. He was very sorry and realized how much of this really was his fault. He apologized profusely and wanted to make it up to her. And she let him.

Well, things were good for awhile, and he seemed to be trying to work things out with her...until...a little time had passed, and he began to turn the tables. Interestingly, his attitude began to change. He not only quit blaming himself, but now all of this was her fault. (It always takes two!) How dare *she* put *him* through this!

After his initial shock had worn off and he knew that he had her back where he wanted her, he not only reverted back to his old intolerable behaviors but now felt justified in doing so and wanted her to pay for the misery she caused him.

Every situation is unique, but generally the underlying theme is the same: When you are in an unhealthy relationship and leave, that's great; but when you leave and then come back thinking things will\ be different, you're in for a surprise. Unless you get professional help or you are fortunate enough to have a partner who is willing to look at himself honestly and want to change, you will return to exactly where you left off...stuck in an unhappy relationship.

I do believe there are some relationships that can and should be worked out. I won't expound on that kind of relationship because that's not what we are dealing with here. Generally you want to leave a relationship you know is bad for you, period. It's that simple. You know in your heart of hearts it's unhealthy. You don't want the same things, and you know it's not going to get any better. *What you see is what you get.* So when you start to entertain the thought of picking up the pieces, there are a few things you can put your money on that will unquestionably happen.

Number One. If you go back, the first three months (some cases more, some less) will be like heaven. He will have actually convinced you he has changed.

Number Two. After the initial re-introduction façade begins to fade, you will start to notice the same old behaviors that made you leave in the first place. Remember: *Zebras don't change their stripes.*

Number Three. You will try again (for the umpteenth time) to fix it, become very depressed and unhappy again, and ask yourself, "*Why* did I come back?"

And finally: **Number Four.** You'll soon find yourself in the exact same situation (minus a couple of valuable months) and realize why you bought this book in the first place.

So if you think you want to go back (which you probably do now, but this will pass if you give yourself time), remember that there were a lot of really good reasons for walking away in the first place. Don't try to pick up the pieces. It's broken. It won't work, it hasn't worked in a long time, and it probably never will. Just give it up. Throw it away, and in time you'll find a new one that you'll like a whole lot better.

Chapter Eighteen

The Do's and Don'ts

Do or do not...there is no try.
— Yoda

COMMON SENSE IS SOMETHING THAT USUALLY GOES OUT
the window when you are trying to end a relationship. The old saying
"Love is blind" isn't totally accurate; it's blind and dumb, too. That's
why you may need someone to lead you by the hand and show you
what you should and shouldn't do. It's easier to see more clearly when
you are on the outside looking in.

So I've made a list to help guide you when you feel as if your
common sense is nowhere to be found.

- Don't call him! Calling him will only set you back and
  postpone the inevitable.
- Do call a friend. Call anyone else but him.
- Don't see him "just one more time" and if you do, don't
  beat yourself up over it.
- Do keep yourself as busy as you can.
- Don't leave any personal belongings at his place so you
  have an excuse to call him or see him. You'll be looking
  for any legitimate excuse when you become desperate,
  or you'll just make one up.

- Don't let him leave anything at your place so he has a reason to come back. Mail it to him.

- Do make a clean break. Even though it's harder this way, you'll be glad you did because it will be easier in the end.

- Don't equivocate. You will second-guess yourself — that's normal — but don't give into it. You will get over this if you give yourself some time.

- Do know that you ended it for a reason. When you play back the tape, play back the whole tape.

- Don't blame yourself. It always takes two. So don't forget it.

- Do learn a lesson from this relationship. This is of extreme importance — you don't want to go through this again, do you? If you don't learn a lesson, you will more than likely make the same mistake again.

- Do get to know yourself better. If you don't, you will be missing out on the best thing in your life — you. Really take the time to find what's in the hidden treasure. If you dig deep enough, you'll be amazed at what you discover.

- Do read and say positive affirmations. Throughout this book, I've mentioned some other books that would also be a good place to start. Also see Recommended Reading on page 133.

- Don't dwell on how it "could've" been. Put your energy to better use — focus on what you want.

- Do look forward to a better future. Once you're beyond this, it will only get better.

- Do forgive and forget. It may not seem possible now, but if you allow yourself this luxury, it will be a gift you give to yourself. It will free you to have a richer future.

- Don't sit around and feel sorry for yourself. Don't allow him to still affect your life even after you've broken it off with him.

- Don't become bitter. He's not worth it. Move on, and you will have a good life. It's your choice.

- Do begin again. Take it one step at a time.

- Do exercise. Do anything physical — force yourself to go to the gym. If you don't belong to one, go for a walk. It's important for you to take care of yourself right now. Even though you don't feel like exercising, this is the one thing that is guaranteed to make you feel better after you do it.
- Do treat yourself to something special. Bubble bath, new hair style, facial, massage, new outfits, dinner, lunch, movie, *anything* — just stay busy.
- Don't give in. You've made the right decision.
- Do allow yourself time to feel better.
- Don't beat yourself up for feeling bad; it's normal. It will pass.
- Don't tell his friends how much you miss him. It will only feed his ego.
- Do what I keep telling you to do! I can't stress it enough. It's a theme throughout this book. It's the key to becoming successful in all areas of your life. It's something that is critically important for you to do: Get to know yourself! Grow. Search. Read. Learn. Read. Think. Explore. Discover. Read. Really delve into finding out more about yourself. Be the best that you can be. Direct your life; don't leave it to chance. You can do anything you set your mind to do; you can become the architect of your future. Do it!

Some of these ideas should keep you on the right path. It's not always easy, but what was easy about staying with what's-his-name? Just think, it might hurt now but in a few months you'll be beyond the hurt. The alternative is that you can stay; and it might hurt now, and in a few months, it will still hurt.

So what was the question? Unfortunately there is no easy way out, but the good news is that there *is* a way out. So take it one day at a time and in time you will be having a great day!

about a
She
th

_____**Chapter Nineteen**_____

This Too Shall Pass

Success is just a matter of luck. Ask any failure.
>   — *Earl Wilson*

WHY CAN'T I STOP THINKING OF HIM? BECAUSE YOU WON'T let yourself! Of course you miss him; you feel horrible. It's inevitable — you're going to feel bad, but *you will get over him*. Even though you don't believe you will, *you will get over him*! There is absolutely, without a doubt, life after what's-his-name. You just have to give yourself time.

Those Friday nights alone when all your friends are busy, sure you are going to feel lonely and sad. So you rent a movie to stay busy and something in the movie reminds you of him, and you end up crying anyway. It's okay, cry — and then dry your tears and tell yourself, "This is normal, and I will feel better soon."

My friend Terri really struggled with this "obsessive thinking of him" thing. She kept telling me that she couldn't get him out of her mind and that she would never get over him. I asked her what she thinks about when she can't stop thinking about him. "Everything," was her response. "Why wasn't I good enough; why doesn't he love me anymore; what did I do wrong?" She said, "I was so good to him. I did everything for him. I loved him so much." And of course, she thought all their times together: vacations, holidays, family stuff, etc. etc.! I didn't let a minute go by that she wasn't directing her thoughts to the past. Terri's biggest problem was that she was missing one major point: She may very well have loved him — but he obviously didn't feel the same about her!

I said, "Hello, Terri, this is your wake up call! Sometimes things just don't work out the way we want them to. So what are you going to do — spend the rest of your life crying over something that's over?" Terri had to come to grips with reality. Her thinking was paralyzing her from moving forward. As she started to gain control of what she thought about all day long, everything else changed, too. There is a saying: "Change the way you look at things, and the things you look at change."

You may have to remind yourself of the fact that old Father Time is on your side. Time is your friend. The more that goes by, the happier you will become. You'll have your good days when you feel like there is hope for you, and then you'll relapse back into sadness and a little depression. Just let it go. *This too shall pass!* Even though you think of him all the time now, as time goes by you will think of him less and less — but it *will* take time.

Don't beat yourself up for having these feelings. You are going through a difficult transition in your life. Letting go is never easy, but just as in the past, you'll look back someday and say, "Thank God for letting me get out when I did."

Remember those other guys you thought that you could never live without? Well, it's the same thing. I know: "But this one is different." And back then, those guys were different, too. Don't forget that you never believed back then that you'd get over them — but miraculously you did. Keep your chin up. Just like a storm that's dark, cloudy, and dreary eventually breaks for bright, sunny, blue skies, so will your time to shine come again. *Believe it, and it will happen.*

Chapter Twenty

If I Could Just Get Him to Love Me Like He Used To

You can always get someone to love you — even if you have to do it yourself.

— *Tom Masson*

I WAS SITTING IN MY THERAPIST'S OFFICE GOING ON AND on about how good my relationship "used to be." I was telling her how thoughtful and considerate he had been and that I was so lucky to have someone who was romantic and affectionate. We used to have so much fun doing nothing together. How could things have changed so much? We had such a great relationship…what happened? I didn't care what happened; whatever it was, I was determined to get him to love me like he used to.

She told me that you don't just get someone to love you. I argued that it was not as if I wanted to get a complete stranger to love me, someone I didn't even know; we had a history together. It had been great between us, and I just wanted to get that back.

She asked me if in the beginning of our relationship I had to "get" him to love me.

I answered, "No...he just did."

She said, "My point exactly. You don't 'get' someone to love you. They either do or they don't. You didn't have to get him to love you then, so why should you have to now?"

That was an eye-opening moment for me. She was right! I didn't have to do anything before — he just loved me. Things were good. I wasn't the one whose feelings changed; he had changed his feelings, and there wasn't anything I could do to change them back.

More importantly, why would I want to? If he didn't love me on his own, I certainly wasn't going to force him to, nor would I want to. What I wanted was the kind of relationship I had before — with someone who loved me the way he used to. Obviously I would have preferred it to be him, but sometimes things just don't work out the way we would like them to. If he loved me, great; but if he didn't, then the last thing I would want to do is twist his arm to get him to love me. What kind of love is that?

This was a turning point for me — realizing that I was worth loving and that I didn't have to *get* someone to love me. When you don't feel worthy of love, you will grab at any crumbs you are thrown. Fortunately for me, the more I learned to love myself the less willing I was to accept those crumbs; as a matter of fact I grew to not even want them anymore.

Mary, a friend of mine, became involved with a wonderful man who literally swept her off her feet. Of course all her closest friends were really happy for her, but at the same time a little leery. It just seemed too good to be true. It wasn't only that he wined and dined her as much as it was that he was very loving in the little ways a woman loves. He would leave little messages for her to find in her suitcase when she traveled; he would tell her all the things that a woman longs to hear but rarely does.

He knew exactly what to say to make her feel good. He really seemed to be perfect for her. Everyone liked him. He was very down-to-earth and a fun person to be around. Even her mother was genuinely happy for her. (Her mother had seen a few jerks come and go.) But this guy was really different…in *all* our objective eyes. In fact, he was the master of treating a woman just the way he should to get her hooked and then once she was hooked, he turned into another person.

Believe it or not he actually had a reason as to why he was now acting so differently, and I must say it did sound legitimate, even to me. He said he couldn't make a commitment until he got his promotion, but after that, they would definitely be together. But lo and behold, he was the Master of Bullshit. He fooled all of us, especially my disappointed-but-still-holding-on-to-his-promises friend. She couldn't understand why things couldn't be the way they were in the beginning. She had a very difficult time letting go, because that dangling carrot seemed to be so real. Unfortunately, she held on to his empty promises until it was so obvious, even to her, that he was not a man of his word.

He got his promotion, but there was no commitment in sight.

Are you in a relationship, trying to do whatever it takes to get noticed? Are you wracking your brain trying to figure out what went wrong and how you can get things back to the way they used to be? Are you trying to please him or possibly trying to get a little bit more of his love? Try no more. Who wants him? He's not worthy of *your* love. If he doesn't want you, someone else will.

Chapter Twenty-one

It's All Going to Be Okay... Everything Is Working Out Just the Way It's Supposed To

We don't receive wisdom; we must discover it for ourselves after a journey that no one can take for us or spare us.

— Marcel Proust

AS TIME GOES ON, SOME OF THE HURT SUBSIDES AND THE memories start to fade. You'll begin to realize that you really are going to be okay. Time not only has a way of healing your wounds, it brings the realization of a brighter future. It's like the first signs of spring popping up after a hard, cold winter. It's something you're really looking forward to, and now that you've survived the worst of it, you'll be able to look forward to a fresh new life.

After dating one man for five years, through all of the ups and downs — his children hating me (his ex told the girls if it weren't for me, their father would come home, which wasn't true, but it made our lives more difficult); his ex always pitting their girls against us, and him taking sides with her instead of me; the long-distance relationship (he lived in Florida and I lived in Pennsylvania), etc. — we decided to get married. The plans were set, the RSVPs were in. Two weeks before the wedding I decided to cancel it.

I was in love with this man, but I knew that it wasn't right, because he just wasn't there for me. My gut was telling me I wouldn't be happy. It wasn't him that I was leaving as much as it was his meddling, always-hanging-on, bitter ex-wife and his unbelievably disrespectful, I'll-do-whatever-it-takes-to-make-your-life-miserable children. It's always a package deal, and this was the deal breaker for me. The situation was out of control, and as hard as I tried, nothing was changing.

I'm telling you this story because at the time I believed I would go to my grave with this man in my heart. I thought I would never get over him. But after some time I began to accept the fact that it was over. As more time went by and some of the pain subsided, I realized that I had survived the worst of it. I began to do a lot of soul searching, and I started to focus on all that was good in my life.

It was then that I can honestly say I knew there was life after what's-his-name. I will always have fond memories of my ex, but I have definitely gotten beyond feeling that I will never be able to live without him. As a matter of fact, not only am I very happy, I am 100% certain that I made the right decision by calling off the wedding. I look back now and am amazed that I didn't leave sooner.

I am a firm believer in "Everything happens for a reason." The hardest part is being patient enough to discover what "the reason" is and learning the lessons that need to be learned. The most difficult times in our lives are when we grow the most. You're a stronger person now. Be good to yourself. And know that everything really does happen for a reason. God has a better plan for you.

Susan Jeffers wrote a great book: *End the Struggle and Dance with Life*. This is a time for you to celebrate. You've come through a hard time, and you have so much to look forward to. So be positive. Do something special for yourself, and be thankful for all that is good in your life. Remember: Gratitude creates happiness. It's simply a matter of where you focus your thoughts.

Part Three

HEALING AND SURVIVING

_____Chapter Twenty-two_____

Fake It 'till You Make It

All glory comes from daring to begin.
> — *Anon.*

YOU'RE SO CLOSE. YOU'RE ALMOST THERE. SOME DAYS YOU actually feel good and then other days you just feel down again. Don't give in to it. Fake it till you make it! Start to *pretend* that you feel good. Take crying, for instance: Try smiling while you are crying. It doesn't work — you can't do both at the same time; so opt for smiling. If you don't feel happy, fake it, and some of it will begin to rub off.

One day I was sitting in my therapist's office crying about how sick and tired I was of feeling bad all the time. Of course, she reiterated that it was my choice and that I was the only one who had control over how I felt. I told her it was hard to feel good when you feel bad. Her response was — then just act...*as if*! This was not her usual professional advice, but she said sometimes it works. Pretend you are an actress playing the part of someone who recently got over their latest love and who is finally beginning to enjoy life again. Start acting *as if* you really do enjoy living. Contemplate what your life will look and feel like when you are where you want to be, and keep your thoughts on the future.

I am by no means suggesting that you live a lie. But have you ever been in a situation in which you felt somewhat unsure of yourself, but you walked in and *acted as if* you were very confident and sure of yourself. You pulled it off, didn't you? You know the saying, "Never let them see you sweat." Well, you can do whatever you put your mind to. Acting *as if* eventually led me to realize that if there were times that I could change the way I was feeling, I really did have control over my moods. It wasn't that the situation was so bad as much as it was what I continued to tell myself about it. If I would dwell on how sad I was, I would be sad. When I chose to think about the good things in my life and put things in perspective, I began to feel better. It truly is all about where you focus your thoughts. Whatever you think, you're right!

We create what we focus on. If you continue to think about what was or how badly you feel, you are not only living in the past but you are also creating more of what you don't want: sadness, guilt, resentment, etc.

You are the only one who has control over your thoughts; no one can do it for you. So start today and try it. The quality of your life is a reflection of what you think about.

Visualization is another great tool. Picture yourself happy again; visualize people telling you how great you look after all you've been through and how happy they are that you aren't with what's-his-name anymore. See yourself in a healthy, happy relationship with someone who really adores you. Picture yourself laughing and smiling and doing the things that you love to do. There are books written on how to visualize. Read one.

Eventually, as you push yourself past this last hurdle, you won't have to fake it anymore. It will no longer be an act; you will have made it on your own. Don't waste another minute of your time feeling bad when you don't have to. Go after your life and live it to its fullest. There is so much out there — you just haven't discovered it yet.

Chapter Twenty-three

What Are You Going to Do Now?

*It does not matter how slowly you go so long as you do
not stop.*

— *Confucius*

NOW IS THE TIME TO DO WHAT EVER YOU HAVE BEEN PUT-
ting off doing while you've been wasting your time crying over what's-
his-name. This is the perfect opportunity to begin to do some of the
things you never allowed yourself the time to do since you were working
your schedule around him. You may feel lost now and not know what
to do with yourself — take this time to really find yourself. Whatever
you do, don't jump right back into another relationship.

Do you even have a clue what your interests are? Many women
wrap their lives so completely around their significant other that it leaves
them very little time to have a life of their own. This is another reason
that when a relationship ends some people fall apart — because they
didn't have a life of their own.

Another thing my mother used to preach to me all the time: "Whatever you do, you have to have your own interests. You can't rely on him
for your happiness; that comes from within. Make sure you have a life

of your own." When I would be down and out, she would always tell me, "*You* make your own good time and *you* make your own bad time." Ultimately, it *is* your attitude that will keep you up or pull you down.

I have a friend who had ended a five-year relationship. She decided that she was going to do the things that *she* had always wanted to do. She bought a horse and really loved it. She even began competing and was becoming a great equestrian — until she met a new guy. Now guess what? She went from riding three times a week to twice a month. She worked her schedule around Mr. Wonderful and at times found herself waiting for him to come home from the golf course (note that *he* didn't give up what he loved doing for *her*). There were many times when he would call and tell her he would be coming home late, so have dinner without him. Of course she would get upset, but the point is that she wouldn't be as upset if she had been out pursuing her *own* interests.

Living your life around a man is the worst possible thing you can do. A women is a lot more attractive to a man if he doesn't think she is dependent on him for every little thing. Anyone who just sits at home waiting for a bone from a man is pretty pathetic. Show him that you don't need him to have a good life. You can be happy with or without him because your life is full. Also, having your own interests makes you more interesting! Let him start to work his schedule around your time, too.

Remember, we teach people how to treat us. When a man thinks that you are there at his beck and call, more than likely he will take you for granted. But if he has to do a little juggling of his time to be with you, then you will be sure to gain a lot more respect from him. And if for some reason the relationship doesn't work out, you still have an interesting life. It makes it whole lot easier to get over someone when you keep yourself busy. An idle mind is the devil's workshop.

Chapter Twenty-four

Your Friends Are Talking But You're Not Listening

*A belief is not merely an idea the mind possesses; it is
an idea that possesses the mind.*

— *Robert Bolton*

WHY IS IT THAT EVERYONE CAN SEE IT BUT YOU? MAYBE
you don't want to admit that they are right because then you would
have to do something about it. Or perhaps you are still making excuses
for his behavior; after all, you understand him better then anyone else.

About fifteen years ago, Debbie, my co-worker, was dating a married man. She was very unhappy. He wouldn't leave his wife and he was
also starting to become physically abusive to Debbie. She said, "But
only on rare occasions." (One time would be enough for me.) I used
to sit with her and beg her to get rid of this guy. I would tell her that if
she gave herself a little time she would be much happier with someone
else. She certainly didn't deserve to be treated the way this man was
treating her.

Did she listen to me? Of course not! He finally divorced his wife,
and Debbie was unlucky enough to marry the jerk. I ran into her years

later, and I asked how everything was going. She proceeded to tell me how unhappy she was and how he demeaned and belittled her all the time. Everything was always her fault, and she would never amount to anything. She started her own business, and instead of encouraging her, he constantly told her she was going to fail.

Unfortunately, now that she realizes that she made a mistake, their ten-year-old son goes berserk every time she mentions leaving. If only she had listened, she would have at least had the chance of having a better life. But instead, she chose to ignore all her friends and family, and now she is paying dearly by living a life of misery.

So many people can tell you exactly the same thing, but until you have had enough, you probably won't listen. There were many times my friends and family would try and tell me how much better off I would be if I would just leave. Once, my girlfriend told me that the next time I dated a man there was a new rule. If anyone of my friends or family began to tell me that this guy wasn't good for me, I had to listen to them and break up with him, even if I didn't want to. It became a joke. But did I listen? Not until I wasted months of my life and cried buckets of tears did I finally do on my own what they had been trying to get me to do all along.

Not listening to the people who love you just doesn't make sense. Do you think they really want to hurt you? Do you believe they just don't want to see you happy with such a wonderful man? Come on, wake up! These are the people who care about you the most, and it hurts them to see you going through what you are going through so unnecessarily. Take your blinders off, step back, and take a good look at the kind of relationship you are in. Are you happy? Is he really all that you make him out to be? Is this really how you want to spend the rest of your life? How does it make you feel to know that you gave your best and it was never good enough?

Since you are struggling with being honest with yourself, allow the people who care most for your well-being to step in and be honest *for* you. When I finally started to listen to my friends and family, I realized that what they were saying was right. I was the one who was wrong.

I was only kidding myself and at the same time hurting myself. Think of it this way...*can they all be wrong?* Are you really the *only* one who can be right? I don't think so. You just happen to be the only one who can't see straight.

Take the rose-colored glasses off and face reality. If you are getting what you want from this man, great. But my guess is you aren't, and that is why you are reading this book.

So if you are not getting what you want, why in the world are you staying in a bad relationship? Come on, get with the program. As they say, "This isn't a dress rehearsal." Make the most of your life, not the least of it. Be strong and do something good for yourself for a change. Walk away when everyone who loves you tells you that you are in a relationship that is bad for you. Life is too short to be miserable. Start to love living; start to look forward to waking up, not dreading what your day will bring. You're playing the game of life all wrong. It's time you start again, and this time, make some new rules.

_____Chapter Twenty-five_____

Don't Do Married Men

Wisdom comes through suffering.
— *Aeschylus*

THIS IS A MISTAKE RIGHT FROM THE VERY BEGINNING —
unless, of course, you don't *want* a real relationship. You are walking
into a house of horrors. *Wake up*! This guy is a cheat, plain and simple.
Oh, don't tell me — he's very unhappily married, right? Well, if he is
so unhappily married, why doesn't he get divorced? Let me guess —
it's really complicated, right? So, then, why would he add *you* to the
equation and further complicate an already messed-up situation? Let
me guess — because he has never met anyone like you. You are so understanding and easy to talk to. You are just so special, aren't you?

Okay, I have one question for you. What makes you think that you
are so special to him that he wouldn't turn around and do the exact
same thing to you if you became his second or third wife! Once a cheat,
always a cheat!

This is one situation that is very difficult for me to understand.
When you involve yourself with a married man, you are setting yourself up for so much heartache and misery. The writing is on the wall.

Who do you think he is going to spend Christmas with? Certainly not you! How about Thanksgiving, Easter, the 4th of July? You know, those really special times during the year when you are sitting alone wondering why you feel so lonely and miserable, settling for so much less than you deserve and actually making excuses for him not being with you. Or how about all the times you have to go *everywhere* solo because the man you chose to love is where he belongs...with his family. If he loves you as much as he says he does, tell him to get a divorce and you will be waiting for him. Then you'll see how fast he moves to prove how serious he really is about you.

Then there is the issue of morals. The fact that your relationship even exists is a real big clue as to what kind of values and morals Mr. Wonderful holds dear. Any man who can deceive his family by having a whole other life is a jerk. And this is the kind of man you want to love? Hellooo-o-o! Speaking of values...where are *yours*? If you were his wife, would you want him making love to another woman? Well, that "other woman" is *you*. What kind of life are you creating for yourself? This isn't a life. It's a measly little piece of one; sharing another woman's husband with her and she gets him on all the fun days. Boy, aren't you lucky? Or, maybe, just stupid.

My friend Caroline had been married to Jim for fifteen years. They did everything with their best friends, Mike and Ali. Jim left Caroline for Ali. Needless to say, Caroline's life was turned upside down, but she eventually got over it. Believe it or not Caroline started dating a married man, Joe, and has been dating him now for seven long years. He has been promising her for all seven years that he is going to get a divorce, and he has yet to file the papers. Why would he get divorced if he doesn't have to? And why would she want to be the other woman? She certainly knew what that felt like.

They break up and get back together at least five times a year, but she still hangs in there, and each time they break up, she swears it's the last. What will it take for her to realize that he is never going to leave his wife? Every holiday, he's with his wife — and they don't even have kids. Caroline is miserable half of her life. It is absolutely mind-boggling to watch a person continue on a path of self-destruction. As long as she stays, she will never experience a real relationship.

This is exactly the reason you should never get involved with someone who is married. You won't have a real life together, only moments that you can steal away (from his wife and children). You won't be able to develop relationships with your family and friends, not to mention his family and friends. You may even have to sneak around so no one sees you together. And God forbid that you get caught.

So if you are dating a married man and wondering why you are so unhappy, wonder no more. No one can sustain themselves on little crumbs thrown to them. It's called "love malnutrition." You can become sick and emotionally die from the lack of wholesome love. So fill your plate with some good healthy lovin', take off that hat, wig, and sun-glasses, and find yourself an *eligible* man with whom you can drink in the joys of life.

Chapter Twenty-six

Don't Do
Separated Men Either

*Whatever games are played with us, we must play no
games with ourselves.*
— *Ralph Waldo Emerson*

ARE YOU THINKING ABOUT GETTING INVOLVED WITH A MAN
who isn't sure about his future — a "separated man"? Well, if you like
to gamble, I can guarantee you one thing: You'll have more fun in Las
Vegas — at least you know your odds there.

Having a relationship with a separated man is unquestionably a
gamble. If he is recently separated or about to be separated, your odds
lessen significantly. This man comes rife with emotional baggage, and
if there are kids involved, well — you might as well hang on tight for
a good roller coaster ride. These guys aren't even remotely ready for
a commitment. They may seem like they are, but that is just a disguise
for their neediness.

This is what I call the classic "rebound relationship." Most men
don't want to be alone and how convenient of you to fill that empty
space for him! Look, none of us really wants to be alone, especially
someone who is "used" to being with someone. But if you want a
healthy relationship and you want to start off on the right foot, this

is my suggestion: This isn't the path to walk down. On the other hand, if you just want a casual affair and have no interest in a commitment; by all means come on board. I'm sure you can both have some fun.

The problems occur when you are strolling along down Lover's Lane and you look to your mate and ask, "When are you going to get a divorce?" You may not know it yet, but you've just opened up a whole new chapter in your relationship. This is when you will begin to realize whether you've hit the jackpot or if you're going home broke.

I first met Sean when I was 28. I had prided myself on never getting involved with a married man. I believed you can't get burnt if you don't jump in the fire. Plus, Sean had been separated for an entire year after a two-year marriage, and his kind-of-ex-wife lived in another state. Seemed safe to me! Oh, and by the way, he was in the process of getting divorced.

After dating him for about a year and a half, I was curious as to exactly when this divorce was going to happen. Guess what he told me? "I'm working on it."

At this point it had been two-and-a-half years since he and his wife separated, and suddenly, out of nowhere, his kind-of-ex-wife wanted to talk about reconciling. To my chagrin and shock, he didn't know what to do. I couldn't believe my ears. We were together 24/7 for two years! We traveled all over Europe. We attended all of his law firm functions together. I would spend holidays with his family and he with mine. We did everything together, and I thought we had a strong, solid relationship.

When I was smacked in the face with all of this, I actually felt like he was having an affair — with his own wife, no less. Boy, was this a rude awakening? The reality was that he was still married and that I was the one who really didn't belong in the picture. But I had allowed this to happen to myself.

After another year of having my life up in the air, not knowing which direction I was going and not wanting to end this relationship, I finally ended it. Do I even have to mention that I *wasted* three years with this guy? (By the way, he never ended up with his ex either.)

Every situation is different, but before heading into this particular kind of relationship, keep your eyes wide open to the fact that "separated" is still "married" no matter how you cut it.

If you like dealing with a lot of headaches and heartaches, there is no question you will find them with a separated man; it just comes with the territory. So, as I mentioned before, "Make a decision about what you want from a relationship and go after it."

If I were gambling on having a good relationship, this isn't the one I would put my money on, no matter what the odds.

Chapter Twenty-seven

The Dust Will Settle

In the midst of winter I finally learned that there was in
me an invincible summer.

— *Albert Camus*

WE ALL FACE ADVERSITY IN OUR LIVES AT ONE TIME OR
another which causes us to deal with very difficult feelings and emotions. It is the manner in which we handle these emotions that deter-
mines our ability or inability to move forward.

Sometimes it's very hard to let go. In the case of the death of
someone we love, there is a part of us that will always hold dear the
love and memories that we shared; this is natural. It is when we are
obsessed and can't move forward that it becomes debilitating to our
emotional growth. (If you are experiencing anything like this, I highly
recommend a therapist to help you through.)

Regardless of the kind of loss, the pain is always greatest in the
beginning. But rest assured, it will subside with time. It is during this
"letting go" process that we suffer so much pain. Often the grief seems
unbearable, but it's critical that you give yourself the time to heal. Time
is the single most important factor that will help you get beyond the
pain.

The beginning of a breakup is like an emotional tornado ripping through your heart. In just a few short minutes, it can be the end of your life as you once knew it, and the devastation can last for months. Once the initial storm has passed and the dust begins to settle, you start to pick up the pieces and put your life back together. It takes time to sort through all of the emotional debris — you must keep the memories that are special and throw out what you can't take with you.

Now is the time to start fresh and build your new life with a strong, healthy foundation. Sure, it's hard to begin again, but what is your alternative? You can live in a place that has been destroyed and try to make a life out of whatever pieces are left or you can make this end a new beginning.

You will begin to see more clearly once you have begun healing from your loss. The dust actually will settle and you will realize that although you have lost something that was very special to you at one time, you've walked away with something even more valuable...a stronger, smarter, and more solid *you*. It is through our most adverse times that our strength of character is built.

You've made it through this nightmare, and you never believed you could. Not only did you survive, but now you can approach life with a fresh new outlook. Every time I have come out on the other end of the tunnel, I am amazed that I made it and that I actually am beginning to feel good again. The road to the end of the tunnel can be long and hard, but keep in mind — you will make it.

I have often wondered why knowing that you will get over someone doesn't make it any easier. I believe this is because it's simply a process that you must go through in order to heal. It's just the way it goes. Eventually you will come out of your darkness.

After the storm has passed, some of the clouds have cleared, and you allow the dust to settle, you will begin to notice the sun shining in your life again. Rebuild your life with all the tools that you have acquired along the way, and you'll have a stronger foundation. You truly are the architect of your life. Make it a good one!

Chapter Twenty-eight

Learn to Forgive

You gain strength, courage and confidence by every experience in which you really stop to look fear in the face. You are able to say to yourself, "I've lived through this horror. I can take the next thing that comes along." You must do the thing you think you cannot do.
                                                        — Eleanor Roosevelt

BREAKING UP WITH SOMEONE YOU LOVE OR LOVED IS NOT easy — even if you wanted it to end, it is still difficult. I'm not going to tell you that it doesn't have to hurt or tell you how easy it is to get over, because we both know that just isn't true. It does hurt — a lot. It's painful, and it is very hard to get beyond. What I am going to tell you is that you *will* survive this. In the beginning, it doesn't seem possible, but when you believe in yourself, you *will* get through that tunnel.

If you allow yourself the time, without this on-again-off-again stuff — you know, the "just let me see you tonight" kind of stuff — and go through the process, you will not only come out of the tunnel but you can come out a stronger, healthier, smarter, and more self-actualized

person. Throughout all this, there are three very important lessons with
which you should walk away.

Lesson #1 — and the most important — is

> **Learn something from this relationship.** *Learn something about
> yourself: how you act in certain situations, how you react, what
> you like about yourself, what you want to change, what you want
> from a relationship, what you don't want, what you are willing to
> put up with, what you won't tolerate.*
>
> *There is something you can walk away from this relationship
> with that is very valuable. Search for it and find it. These are the
> lessons in life. This is how you grow, get to know yourself better,
> and become stronger. No one is perfect. We all make mistakes.*

Which brings me to Lesson #2:

> **Forgive yourself!** *If you've made mistakes — or should I say when
> you make mistakes — forgive yourself, and go on. There is nothing
> you can do now to change the past, but the good news is you can
> affect your future. You can do this by not allowing yourself to make
> the same mistakes again, and even if you do, forgive yourself
> again, because eventually you will get it right.*
>
> *Forgiving yourself allows you to be your own friend. It takes
> pressure off you for not being perfect, and it gets rid of guilt. Forgive-
> ness is a gift you give yourself. You must learn to forgive yourself
> before you can truly learn to forgive others.*

Which brings us to Lesson #3:

> **Forgive him.** *I know this may seem impossible to you right now,
> but, hopefully, someday you will allow yourself to get to this point.
> You don't have to forgive him right now — or ever for that matter
> — but if and when you do, you'll be a better person for it. When
> you don't forgive him, you hold on to him. (And wouldn't he be
> happy to know that?) You will carry anger and resentment around
> with you wherever you go. (Who needs that?)*
>
> *Harboring such negative emotions and thoughts turns you
> into a bitter, resentful person. It zaps you. You forfeit living the
> positive, quality life you deserve. The more negative energy and
> anger you choose to live with, the harder it is to enjoy today. It
> will permeate most areas of your life. Why would you want to live*

with a negative aura like that? Is he worth it? If you are not going
to forgive him, you might as well go back with him because he is
still making your life miserable. Why? Because you're allowing it!

When I first met Mark, he had been separated for about 2½ years after a 16-year marriage. He worked in sales and was on the road in Miami when one night he called home and his wife informed him that she wasn't in love with him anymore and that when he returned home she wanted him to move out.

Needless to say, he was devastated — he got into his car and drove twenty hours home to Jackson, Mississippi. One of the main reasons he didn't want his marriage to end was because of his two young daughters and what they would have to live through. He tried to keep things together to no avail, and eventually he moved out.

As he was struggling to put his life back on track, he met a woman and fell in love. At the same time, his ex-wife decided she wanted him back. Although he struggled with his decision, ultimately he decided not to go back home.

He was extremely generous — both financially and with his time — to his ex-wife and their children. He was the kind of ex-husband most women would die for. Unfortunately, his ex-wife didn't think so. She became a woman scorned since now that she wanted him back he wasn't running back to her. What was even more unfortunate was that she became very bitter, and she used the children to get back at him every chance she could.

She couldn't forgive herself for making a mistake, and she couldn't forgive him for not coming back home. She not only made herself very miserable but she put a wedge between her children and their father that is irreparable. Her resentment caused her to use her own children as pawns in a sad, unwarranted no-win war.

By not forgiving, you not only hurt yourself with indelible wounds, but you may unwittingly destroy the people you love the most. Dwelling on revenge and resentment causes you to stay mired in negativity, and your life will reflect it. This situation, like so many others, could have had a much more equitable outcome for all involved if only there could have been forgiveness.

Once you find forgiveness, you will regain control of your life and step off the emotional roller coaster. The result will be a more peaceful and harmonious life. You are the only one who can decide in which direction your life will go.

Instead of focusing on all the ways you can get back at him, put your attention on how you can get your *own* life back to where you want it to be. Get in control of your life; you are the only one who can. He's out of your life now, so keep him there and move on. I know it's not easy, but it can be done, so what are you waiting for? Start today to make *you* the most important person in your life, not what's-his-name. It simply is not worth your time and energy. Pain is inevitable; suffering is optional.

Chapter Twenty-nine

Live in the Present

What a wonderful life I've had! I only wish I'd realized it sooner.

— Colette

SPENDING YOUR TIME THINKING ABOUT WHAT COULD'VE been or thinking "I should've said this or done that ... if only I had ... I wish I had one more chance to say ...." If, if, if, shoulda, woulda, coulda. We all do it, and we're all guilty of wasting a lot of precious time doing it. These thoughts are only useful when you are analyzing in your mind how you could've handled things differently. You can then learn from your mistakes and find out how your behavior contributed to some of the problems so that you can avoid making the same mistakes in the future.

To continually fill your mind with thoughts of the past and things that are over and done with is futile. You can't change the past. So, learn from it, then — *let it go*. I know that it's easier said than done but — *you can do it*!

I am lucky enough to have great friends that I can lean on in times of need, and as they well know there have been many times when I've needed them. Years ago, when I had just ended a four-year relationship and I was working with my friend Joni, I just couldn't stop thinking about or talking about Greg. Everything reminded me of him. I would reminisce about a good time we had together and laugh. Then, the next minute I'd be crying. I was clearly stuck in the past. I believed that if I had said things differently or done things differently, maybe things would have worked out for us.

As any good friend would, Joni commiserated with me, held my hand, listened to me, and dried my tears. After the second day, she told me that I had to get hold of myself and stop thinking of him. Of course I said, "But I can't."

And she said, "Yes, you can, but *you* are not allowing yourself." I asked her how she proposed I just stop thinking of someone who has been a major part of my life for four years. She told me that every time I think of him I had to say an affirmation and refocus my thoughts to something else instead of dwelling on the past. It sounded impossible to me, and at first it was difficult, but with a little practice I found that she was right. Instead of trying to change something I couldn't — the past — I changed the only thing that I could, and that was the way I was thinking. I began to control my thoughts instead of allowing my thoughts to control me.

Every time you start to think about him, repeat these words: "Thank you, God (Allah, Mohammed, Higher Power, Whomever), for getting me out of an emotionally unfulfilling situation." Even if you don't believe it now, if you repeat it enough times, you will begin to believe it. Next thing you know, you will be out of an emotionally unhealthy relationship that was not fulfilling your needs.

Remember, when you waste your time living in yesterday, you miss out on today. As hard as it may be at times, try to make every day a good day. Every day you will get a little bit better.

There are lots of things that you have to be thankful for — just open your eyes and look around you. Don't take for granted what you've been blessed with. Since you love to dwell on things, dwell on what's good. When you find yourself drifting into negative, woe-is-me thinking, say out loud, "Stop it!" Then replace those thoughts with whatever you have in your life to be grateful about: your health, your children, your sight, your ability to talk, your ability to walk, your home, furniture, car, mother, father, friends, job, etc. Many people have it a lot worse than you do. I know that may not diminish your pain, but it should help to put it in perspective.

The good news is that you can eventually let go of the past, and being a lot smarter, you can enter into your next relationship knowing more of what *you* want. You will actually begin to get your needs met. Wouldn't that be a change? A welcome one, to say the least!

There's an old adage: "You can't get where you're going looking in the rear view mirror." Yesterday is gone. Take from the past what you can use to make a better future — *"the lessons you've learned"* — and leave the rest behind — it's useless. It doesn't do you any good to rehash something you can't change, and it wastes your energy.

I know a lot of what I'm saying may seem impossible for you to do right now, but believe me, having lived through the pain myself, I know that you can and will get over it. So quit wasting your time living in the past. Keep your mind focused on the "present" — it's a gift you give yourself.

Chapter Thirty

Who Am I? Where Am I? And How Did I Get Here?

Growth demands a temporary surrender of security.
— Gail Sheehy

HAVE YOU EVER SAT AND WONDERED HOW YOU GOT WHERE you are in your life right now? Have you ever thought about how many choices you have made along the way and how they have changed your life?

And why do you think you made certain choices instead of others? Every single choice takes you down a different path, so make sure you really think about what you want to choose for your life.

I have made a lot of really bad personal choices — some I have painfully regretted. Others I made because I was too young and didn't have the wisdom to make smarter ones. I have often sat and wondered how regretting these decisions is beneficial to me other than learning not to make the same mistakes again. I must admit that I've wasted a lot of time wishing that I had done things differently, but to my dismay, all my fretting over what has passed only made me continue to make my past a very big part of my present. It is like living with a ghost: It's there, but it really isn't.

Stop regretting the mistakes that you have made and move on. If you don't, you might relive them so many times that it would be like living in a time warp. Haven't you paid long enough? Knowing that you are not perfect and that it's okay to make mistakes allows you to quit blaming yourself. I think this is a very difficult thing for most people to do. We are always the hardest on ourselves.

A turning point of real growth is when you begin to realize that your life is whatever *you* decide to make it and that you actually have the ability to change your life. Growth entails change, and for many, change is both scary and unnerving. Leaving something that you have become accustomed to can be very unsettling, even when your desire is to move forward in your life.

Staying with what is familiar doesn't have any risk. You're safe even if you aren't satisfied. Why do you think so many people stay in dead-end relationships or jobs that they can't stand going to everyday? Most likely because they are afraid to fail! What if you put forth the effort that is needed to make a real change in your life and you don't like where it takes you? Generally, when you push yourself to change a situation that you aren't happy with, the mere fact that you have the strength and courage to take such a step is very critical in building self-esteem. You may not like where it takes you, but you will be more self-assured because you have accomplished something you had been afraid to try — and you now know that you can change your circumstances when you choose to do so.

Getting beyond your fears can open doors to so many new possibilities. When fear holds you back from taking a step forward, it will not only keep you hopelessly stuck right where you are, but it also does very little to build your opinion of yourself.

I can't tell you how much my life has changed in the last year because I finally got beyond some of my fears and made some changes that were very challenging. Just the fact that I was willing to go out on a limb and face the unknown made me feel more confident and gave me strength to attempt even more. It's like a snowball effect: The more you do, the stronger you get; and the stronger you become, the more you are capable of doing. But if you don't try it, you'll never know.

Fear is the opposite of faith. It is all about where you place your focus. So many of us waste our lives being afraid of what turns out to be nothing. I believe that what you dwell on will actually manifest itself in your life, like a self-fulfilling prophecy. Negative thinking begets negativity, and the opposite is also true. You can retrain your mind to stop the negative thoughts and replace them with positive thinking. It takes a lot of work, and you have to have a very strong desire to want to change the direction of your life.

So when you wake up and ask, "How did I get here?" you now know that *you* brought yourself here with the choices that you have made and the kind of thinking with which you constantly fill your head. No one ever said it was going to be easy, but it's a lot easier than you think — *you* just have to take the first step.

There are two ways that people can look at themselves: through their own opinion of themselves or through the opinion of others. The most important thing is the feelings they have about themselves. Do you like who you are? Do you even know what there is to like about you? Do you believe that you are confident, intelligent, sexy, friendly, giving, etc.? Whatever you believe about yourself subconsciously will become a part of your personality.

If you don't feel worthy or you don't like who you are, you'll be sure to attract someone who feels the same way about you. In some uncanny way, what you believe about yourself will somehow shine through. For instance, how you allow others to talk to you or treat you is a major factor in determining your sense of self. If you let people talk down to you or walk all over you, it is a clear indication that you have a low self-opinion. On the other hand, if you set boundaries and expect to be treated with respect, it's a sign that you have high self-esteem. So where you are in your life *right now* is a direct reflection of your opinion of yourself and what you fill your head with all day. We make our decisions and choices based on what we believe we are worth.

Begin to listen to what you say to yourself. If it's bad, change it! Start to pursue new interests. Set goals and, more importantly, realize that you are truly worthy of your heart's desires. Make a commitment to become the person you've longed to be, and take your life in whatever direction you choose.

Chapter Thirty-one

Cultivate Yourself

*If we have not peace within ourselves, it is in vain to
seek it from outward sources.*
— *François de la Rochefoucauld*

JUST IN CASE YOU STILL DON'T QUITE UNDERSTAND THE
magnitude of what really getting to know yourself can do for you, I'm
going to talk to you about this *again*.

It is absolutely imperative that you start this journey now!

If you don't, you will more than likely find yourself involved in another
unhealthy relationship similar to the one you're struggling with letting
go of right now. My guess is that's the last thing that you want to have
happen, but believe me, if you don't do a little research and inves-
tigative work into what makes you tick, that's exactly where you will
end up.

Besides, when you finally *do* invest the time to learn about yourself, you will be glad that you did. You'll be writing me to thank me
for adding another chapter on this topic.

It's time to focus on you and what makes you unique. Dig deep inside and find out what it is that you want from life; then go after it. Get out of your rut and move on!

Allow me to list some of the Pros of taking the time to find out about yourself and a few of the Cons of not taking the time for getting to know yourself.

Pros:

- You will meet the best friend that you will ever have.
- You will start to recognize the mistakes you've made and why — so you won't make them again.
- You will be kinder to yourself.
- You will regain your self-esteem, or perhaps you'll begin to realize that you have self-esteem.
- Let me say that again: You will, without a doubt — unquestionably — rebuild your self-esteem.
- You will realize that you are lovable and desirable.
- In the next relationship, you will be far less likely to put up with any behavior that's disrespectful.
- You will be a stronger person.
- You will be a smarter person.
- You will know *your* likes and dislikes.
- You will recognize if your needs are being met and you will have new boundaries.
- You will choose a healthier mate the next time.
- You will have a more positive outlook on life.
- You won't feel like crying all the time.
- You will enjoy life for a change. You will like living.
- You will find that your worth comes from within and not through a man.

Cons:

- You will attract the same kind of mate.
- You will make the same mistakes.
- You may never find what truly makes you happy.
- You will continue to suffer from low self-worth.
- You won't like yourself as much.
- You will continue to struggle with and probably fail in other relationships.
- You will never know how truly great you are (what a major loss!)
- You will probably feel bad a lot in your relationships.
- You will continue to blame yourself when things go wrong.
- You won't get *your* needs met (and that is a tragedy).
- You will miss out on having a fuller, healthier life.
- You won't have as much fun living.
- You will miss out on meeting the best friend in your life.
- You will verbally abuse yourself.
- You will be weak and unhealthy emotionally.
- You will feel like you are just going through the motions in life.
- You will never know how to have boundaries.

You can see now why it's worth the effort. I would assume there isn't a question *whether* you will begin, but *when* you will begin (right now!). As Nike says, "Just Do It!" — unless, of course, you *like* being in this kind of relationship or you like being miserable, which I seriously doubt. Yet somehow we continue to repeat the same familiar patterns, and our choices end up being painful mistakes.

You may even discover that some of your unhappiness wasn't because of your relationship but because of your inability to love yourself. By allowing yourself the opportunity to know yourself better — thereby growing and becoming healthier — you can avoid walking down the path where Mr. Wrong lives and choose a more compatible mate. Believe me, it does take work to discover what you've kept buried and hidden away for so long, but once you find and begin to uncover this treasure, not only will you be amazed at some of your strengths and talents that you've buried away for so long, but you will feel like a prisoner who has just been set free from a long, tortuous captivity and taking the first steps to a wonderful new life.

Investing the time to grow with yourself will be the greatest and most rewarding investment that you will ever make. So take this time to get to know the most precious thing that God has given you — *yourself* — and you'll be thankful you did.

Chapter Thirty-two

Freedom of Choice

We who lived in concentration camps can remember the
men who walked through the huts comforting others,
giving away their last piece of bread. They may have
been few in number, but they offer sufficient proof that
everything can be taken from a man but one thing: the
last of human freedoms — to choose one's attitude in
any given set of circumstances — to choose one's way.
— Viktor Frankl

WHERE DO YOU WANT YOUR LIFE TO GO FROM HERE? IF YOU
believe you can, you can take your life in any direction you *choose*.

First you have to quit feeling sorry for yourself. This is a biggie.
Don't let me give you the wrong idea, I'm not saying that you can't
feel sorry for yourself — the beginning of the breakup is the only time.
It's important that you allow yourself to feel the pain. My guess is that
you will probably do the usual amount of wallowing and then some.
This is a good thing; feel it and then — let it go.

The key here is in letting it go. Believe it or not, this is a choice
— you either make up your mind to move on or you choose to continue harboring thoughts of him. Either way, it's a choice you make.
I've heard people say, "I just can't let go." Change *can't* to *won't*...
because you *can* when you *choose* to.

I know this has been difficult for you, but let me try and put this in perspective. Would you rather be hurting from this or mourning over the death of someone you love (and who actually loved you back)? Would you rather be crying over this or crying because you just found out you have a terminal illness? This is serious stuff here! You're crying over someone who makes your life more difficult and who isn't there for you. The problem is that sometimes we just don't realize how much good we have in our lives, and we keep our attention focused on what is bad or what is not working in our lives.

We take so much of the good for granted and dwell on the negative. It's time to change your focus. It's time to get yourself a great life and develop a positive attitude — which brings me to another choice that we have. Your attitude: It can make you or break you. It's more important than just the facts. You can't control other people or change the past, but you can change your attitude. Do it! Don't live in the past. It's over and done with and now you have the opportunity to begin again with less chance of making the same mistakes.

I am here to tell you how lucky you are to be out of such a miserable relationship. At least now you have a chance. There is a whole new world that's open to you. Live your life to the fullest; this is the only chance you get. There is no going around twice. Quit taking the blessings in your life for granted and quit thinking that he was one of them. If that were true, you wouldn't be going through this right now.

There were times when I was going through the "mourning process" that I would feel so depressed that I just couldn't let go. Even my friends were telling me that enough is enough; you just have to get over this guy. But I continued to hold on to "what could've been" and "if only" — I would spend countless hours wondering whether if I had acted differently perhaps things would've worked out better. Now that I'm over whatever-his-name-was at the time, I cringe over all the precious time I wasted thinking I could change something that I had absolutely no control over. Now I'm even glad that it's over.

Life is too short to worry about something that you can't change and something that you will ultimately be glad happened anyway. With each and every relationship I've walked away from, in the beginning I thought I could never get over him, but now, in retrospect, I'm glad it ended. If I hadn't walked away, I would still be living in a miserable relationship and wouldn't have been able to attain the level of self-actualization, happiness, and fulfillment that I now enjoy.

Please give yourself a chance — you're worth it. Your life can be so much more than memories and self-pity. You have the advantage of starting over, so where do you want your life to go? It's your choice!

Chapter Thirty-three

Do Yourself the Biggest Favor of Your Life: Get to Know Who You Are

The tragedy of life is not so much what men suffer, but rather what they miss.

— *Thomas Carlyle*

YOU'VE BEEN *SO* CONSUMED WITH WHAT'S-HIS-NAME AND all the *whys* of your relationship that it has left you very little time to cultivate a relationship with yourself. Knowing yourself better and liking yourself are fundamental components of self-esteem. Unfortunately, the fact that you've stayed in an unhealthy relationship and allowed it to continue even when you knew you shouldn't is evidence that you are suffering from, shall we say, a shortage of self-esteem.

That's the bad news. The good news is that you're moving forward and actually doing what it takes to begin the process of developing higher self-esteem. You left! Isn't that exciting?! You can now take the time to become a better you. It's like you are going on an adventure and exploring unknown areas. Take this time to expand your self-awareness. Make a commitment to learn about yourself with the end result being a better, stronger, and more confident you.

Our actions and thoughts significantly determine our level of self-esteem. When you allow yourself to be treated badly, abused, disrespected, treated inconsiderately, yelled at, talked down to — whatever applies to your situation — you betray yourself and your self-esteem suffers. *Self-respect* is your belief in your own worth, belief that your life and your well-being have value, and belief that you deserve to be respected by others. Your personal fulfillment and contentment are important enough to work toward.

A very close friend of mine has never taken the time to really get to know herself. She believes that she has learned from each relationship and swears that she will never make the same mistakes again, but she inevitably ends up in the same kind of relationship crying over some sort of behavior that she eventually realizes she just can't live with.

She never takes time between relationships to sit back and be by herself. She jumps from one immediately into another. If she would only allow herself the time to analyze what makes her stay in unhappy relationships, then she could recognize the signs and stop herself from repeating those mistakes. She may also come to understand why she has to have someone all the time and why she just can't be alone.

It wasn't until recently that she decided to see a therapist. It was brought to her attention that one of the biggest mistakes that she makes in her relationships is that she never speaks up if something is bothering her. She believed that if she talked about what she didn't like in the relationship, she would lose the person. Unfortunately, the men in her life are not mind readers, and they aren't even aware that anything is wrong.

Because she is afraid to put her cards on the table, she will never give herself the chance of getting her needs met. One of the reasons she allows these men to walk all over her without saying anything is that she doesn't place as much value on herself as she does on the men in her life. This shows an obvious lack of self-worth. She doesn't seem to know that *her* feelings are important, too. If he should decide to walk away because she wants to negotiate a more equitable arrangement then he wasn't worth it in the long run. It's not always easy to look at how you contribute to the fall of a relationship, and it's impossible to see it if you won't even take the time to look for it.

This is a time for setting goals, letting go of the past, and looking forward to a bright new future. So let's start. You may have asked yourself why this happened. This is the evidence that everything happens for a reason — the reason being that you will walk away from this relationship with valuable knowledge, a stronger sense of self-worth, and an awareness of what truly is important to you.

Get out a piece of paper and a pencil and answer these questions: What is most important to me? What drives me in my life? What's most important in a job, a relationship, a friendship? What are my values? What beliefs limit me the most? What are my goals? Am I positive or negative? What are some of the areas of my life where I'm dissatisfied? How can I change them? What makes me happy? What makes me sad? What motivates me? Think of your own questions. Really delve inside yourself and find out who you are and what you truly want from life.

You'll be sure to find some things you don't like, but now you will be able to recognize them and begin to work on them to improve yourself. You'll also begin to know yourself like never before. There are many great books written on self-esteem, ending the struggle and moving forward. Just go to any library or bookstore and sit in the self-help section. You'll find something that appeals to you.

A lot of people take the time to work out to have a better body. They take the time to go to college to be better educated. They take the time to shop and have better clothes. But they won't take the time to get to know themselves better, to become a better person. They don't know what they are missing.

As you begin your journey, push aside doubt and know that wherever you are going will be better than where you've been. I'm not going to tell you that it's easy. It's not. But if you put forth the effort, the rewards of how it will enrich your life will be worth all the energy you expend. So jump on the bandwagon. Take your time, and take the time to do what it takes to excel. You'll be happy you did.

Chapter Thirty-four

If You Can't Find Your Way, Turn on the Light

Never think that God's delays are God's denials. Hold
on; hold fast; hold out. Patience is Genius.
— *Comte de Buffon*

WHEN YOU DON'T KNOW WHERE YOU ARE GOING, WHY
don't you just ask for directions? When you are fumbling around in
the dark trying to find your way, why don't you just turn on the light?
We mortals try to do things by ourselves and always screw things up.
When you make God a partner in your life and put Him in the drivers'
seat, you'll find out how to get there.

This may be an optional chapter for those of you who like to go
it alone. I certainly would never want to push my spiritual beliefs on
you, but for those of you who are interested, there is something I'd like
to say: When you have faith in God, you can let go of worry and fear.
Fear *is* the opposite of faith. When you are afraid that you will never
meet anyone again or when you are afraid that you have made a mistake or if the fear is overwhelming that you won't be able to make it
on your own, trust that God is taking you in the right direction, and
with prayer, you will make it to where you want to be.

Pray for God's guidance, and He will show you the way. There have been countless times that I saw the signs in my relationships that said, "Exit here," and instead of leaving I chose to stay. God showed me the signs, and I chose to ignore them. He gave me the opportunity to leave, but my choice was to stay and continue to try and make things work in a relationship that wasn't working.

You might ask yourself, "Why did God put me in this kind of a situation?" God didn't put you there, you did. God gives us the opportunity to choose. He has given us freedom of choice. *We* choose what situations we put ourselves into, and if you find yourself somewhere you really don't want to be, leave. It is up to us to truly believe and to know — unquestionably — that when we pray for His guidance, He will give it to us, through either that gut feeling, our intuition, or little signs.

At times, the signs are there loud and clear for you to see, but because you are still trying to control the situation and get the outcome you want, you refuse to see reality. Resisting what "is" causes a struggle to ensue. It can affect every aspect of your life, resulting in a lot of heartache and turmoil.

Sometimes you just have to trust that it wasn't meant to be. All the signs are there staring you in the face — open your eyes and take a good hard look at what you see. I believe there is a reason for everything. Maybe it was to learn a lesson. Maybe it was so you could teach a lesson. And sometimes, we may never know the reason.

Let God be God. Let Him guide you and be smart enough to listen to what He is trying to tell you. Be quiet enough to hear what He is saying to you. Meditate. It is God in all areas of your life making things happen at the right time and in the right way.

There were many times that I asked God why He was doing this to me when He knew how much I loved what's-his-name. I would cry my eyes out praying that He would please make things work out for us. Of course, I thought I knew what was best for me. Even though I didn't know it at the time, things actually were working out for the best.

I believed with all my heart that this was the man for me, and I wanted more than anything for this relationship to last. It took me a while to realize that He was right and I was wrong. Well, guess what? If I had listened to what God was trying to tell me in the beginning and taken notice of the signs, I would've saved myself a lot of time and heartache.

When you can't find your way in the dark, turn to God, and He will always light your path. Whenever you start to feel bad and begin to worry, remember that God *is* showing you the way and that everything is working out just the way it is supposed to.

Chapter Thirty-five

Conclusion: The End — It's Just the Beginning!

When one door of happiness closes, another opens; but often we look so long at the closed door that we do not see the one which has been opened for us.
— Helen Keller

THE ONLY THING THAT REMAINS CONSTANT IN LIFE IS change. Everything changes from one minute to the next. It's when you grasp this concept that you truly begin to appreciate life. (A good book to help you understand this philosophy is *It's Easier Than You Think* by Sylvia Boorstein.) Sometimes change is welcome, and other times change is really a struggle. But in knowing that everything changes, your struggle will change into enlightenment and growth.

Ending a relationship, leaving someone you love, and letting go is painful and difficult — but it can and has been done. I know from my own painful mistakes how truly hurtful it can be. I have also come to learn that not only is it survivable, but if you are willing to allow yourself to learn and grow from these losses, what you actually gain from them is far more valuable than you've yet to realize. I truly hope that what I've imparted to you through this book will help you to discover yourself, and in so doing, raise yourself to a new level of personal development and fulfillment.

I hope that when there may not be anyone else to talk to, you can reach for this book as guidance, inspiration, and a friend to boost you up when you're feeling down. I wrote this book to let you know that you are *not* going crazy, that it *wasn't* all your fault, and that all of the various stages you are going through are merely normal feelings in the process of letting go.

But more importantly, I pray that you walk away from this book with the desire and motivation to want to truly learn about yourself and find out what it is you want from life — and then to have the courage and discipline to go after it. This experience has caused you a lot of heartache and pain, so let it be your greatest teacher.

Your future is yours and yours alone to create. So live in the peace of knowing that you are getting beyond the pain — *you really will make it through this* — and once you've made it through that proverbial tunnel, the light you see will be filled with love, a healthier, happier you, and the kind of relationship that you so richly deserve.

God Bless You.

Go placidly amid the noise and the haste, and remember what peace there may be in silence. As far as possible without surrender, be on good terms with all persons. Speak your truth quietly and clearly and listen to others, even the dull and ignorant; they too have a story. Be yourself. Especially do not feign affection. Neither be cynical about love — for in the face of all aridity and disenchantment it is as perennial as the grass. Take kindly the counsel of the years, gracefully surrendering the things of youth. Nurture strength of spirit to shield you in sudden misfortune. But do not distress yourself with imaginings. Many fears are born of fatigue and loneliness. Beyond a wholesome discipline, be gentle with yourself. You are a child of the universe no less than the trees and the stars; you have a right to be here. And whether or not it is clear to you, no doubt the universe is unfolding as it should. Therefore be at peace with God, whatever you conceive Him to be, and whatever your labors and aspirations, in the noisy confusion of life keep peace with your soul. With all its sham, drudgery and broken dreams, it is still a beautiful world.
— From the works of Max Ehrmann

Recommended Reading

The Power of Your Sub-Conscious Mind — Dr. Joseph Murphy

The Powermind System — Michael Monroe Kiefer, M.S.

It's Easier Than You Think — Sylvia Boorstein

Transform Your Life — Rev. Dr. Barbara King

Discover the Power Within You — Eric Butterworth

Choose to Live Peacefully — Susan Smith Jones, Ph.D.

End the Struggle and Dance With Life — Susan Jeffers Ph.D.

The Feeling Good Handbook — David D. Burns, M.D.

The Six Pillars of Self-Esteem — Nathaniel Branden

Do It! Let's Get Off Our Buts — Peter McWilliams

Soul Love — Sanaya Roman

Awaken the Giant Within — Anthony Robbins

Excuse Me, Your Life Is Waiting — Lynn Grabhorn

The Power of Intention — Dr. Wayne W. Dyer

The Science of Mind — Ernest Holmes

You Can Heal Your Life — Louise L. Hay

The Power Is Within You — Louise L. Hay

In the Meantime: Finding Yourself and the Love You Want — Iyanla Vanzant

The Magic of Thinking Big — David Schwartz, Ph.D.

Life Strategies: Doing What Works, Doing What Matters — Phillip C. McGraw, Ph.D.

Man's Search for Meaning — Victor Frankl

Attitude Is Everything — Keith Harrell

The Game of Life and How to Play It — Florence Scovel Shinn

Susan Russo

SPEAKER
AUTHOR
TRAINER

Susan is a gifted, dynamic, and inspirational speaker and trainer.

Susan's topics include
- ❥ Change Your Mind, Change Your Life
- ❥ Goal Setting
- ❥ Getting Over What's-His-Name

For more information, visit *www.pinnaclethought.com*

For booking information, contact
Pinnacle Thought Inc.
3110 Annandale Drive
Presto, Pennsylvania 15142
Phone: 412-278-1611
Email: *info@pinnaclethought.com*

There Is Life After What's-His-Name gave me the COURAGE to do some long overdue soul searching about my relationship. It is the first step for any woman who has yet to realize her worth!
J. Dreyer, *New Jersey*

Finally, someone that will tell me like it is and not just how I want to hear it. I realized reading this book that my relationship was worth saving — I just desperately needed to set some boundaries.... Thanks, Susan!
L. Kerr, *Florida*

Reading your book has made me take my head out of the sand and realize that I deserved so much more... never again will I waste my time in unhealthy relationships. Thank you for the knowledge and [for] sharing all your experiences. I'm now ready to move on to a better life.
Sherry M., *Pittsburgh*